tools for cooks

Christine McFadden
photography by Mark Williams

tools
for
cooks

foreword by Anne Willan

jacqui
small

This book is dedicated to my father

First published in 2000 by Jacqui Small,
an imprint of Aurum Press Ltd, 25 Bedford Avenue, London WC1B 3AT

Reprinted in 2000

Publisher Jacqui Small
Editorial Director Stuart Cooper
Art Director Robin Rout
Food Stylist Pippin Britz
Photoshoot Production Assistant Josie
Frater
Production Geoff Barlow

British Library
Cataloguing-in-Publication Data
A catalogue record for this book is
available from the British Library

ISBN 1-903221-00-5

Printed and bound in Hong Kong

RECIPE NOTES

Pan sizes
Where possible, use the size and shape
of pan specified in the recipe, otherwise
the cooking time or the amount of
liquid may need adjusting. In the recipe
tools lists, the terms 'small', 'medium'
and 'large' refer to the following sizes:

Frying pans
small 18–20cm diameter
medium 22–26cm diameter
large 28–30cm diameter

Saucepans
small 1.3–1.8 litres
medium 2–3 litres
large 4–5 litres

Spoon measurements
These refer to standard measuring spoons rather
than table cutlery, which varies in capacity. All spoon
measurements are level.

Herbs and spices
Herbs are fresh unless dried herbs are specified. Chillies are
fresh unless dried chillies are indicated. Spices and seeds are
whole unless ground are specified.

Oils
If a recipe requires vegetable oil, use a light oil with a neutral taste, such as
sunflower, grapeseed, safflower or groundnut. Blended oils and corn oil are
not recommended. If 'olive oil' is indicated, use 'pure' olive oil – a blend of
refined and extra-virgin oils. Use 'extra-virgin' oil only when specified.

Other ingredients
Vegetables are medium-sized unless otherwise indicated. Eggs are large.

contents

foreword

A fine tool is a treasure. It curves to the hand, balanced, ready for action. With the right tool, egg whites are whisked in a matter of moments and stones pop from olives. Zest curls crisply from the rind of an orange, with a titillating puff of citrus to the nose. Where would a genoise be without its cake tin, or a fine sauce without a conical strainer? Thanks to the classic black frying pan, an omelette cooks and rolls almost effortlessly onto the plate, so carefully are the sides angled and the handle designed. My own favourite is the mandoline slicer – even the name is an inspiration – which whittles potatoes and other roots so effortlessly into perfect slices, julienne strips, latticed waffles, even dice if you make the right manoeuvre.

Don't get me wrong. I'm not talking about gadgets. Like any serious cook I hate those cheap cutters and plastic gizmos that are touted with such dexterity on the supermarket aisles. They clutter up the kitchen drawer and, as often as not, break the first time you use them. No, what I have in mind are those robust, timeless tools that simplify the cook's life and are built to last – the heavy copper pans, the sturdy rolling pins. My balance scales, for instance, are at least 100 years old and must once have belonged to a shopkeeper as the brass pans are stamped with the yearly assay to prove their accuracy. They weigh 5 kilos of merchandise or more to the nearest 5 grams – what electronic marvel does the same?

Treasures do not always come cheap, though one of my most useful implements is a simple metal skewer that I use as a primitive meat thermometer. Most of all, I think of knives, the fundamental tool of any cook. A good knife knows its owner – the grip is polished and worn to accommodate an individual hand. The blade, kept sharp with loving care, performs tasks almost instinctively under its master's guidance. Both work in harmony to achieve miracles of precision and speed.

All these and many other implements are presented in this informative, accurate and well thought-out book. *Tools for Cooks* demonstrates that a fine tool is one of the great pleasures of life, both inside and outside the kitchen.

Anne Willan

introduction

There was a time not so very long ago when the home cook had to search for kitchen tools in dusty hardware shops or make do with the limited selection offered by department stores. If you were more enterprising, you could venture into one of those awe-inspiring but impersonal shops that supply chefs and caterers. Nowadays, the choice of kitchen tools and cookware has proliferated beyond belief. Along with cook books and TV cookery shows, there is an abundance of cookshops, specialist mail order companies and websites, from which an astonishing range of kitchenware can be purchased. Along with quantity, quality has improved too. Knives, pots and pans come in sleek designs and state-of-the-art materials.

While there is no shortage of choice, there is a lack of accessible information on how and what to choose. For example, how do you find

As well as detailed information on tools and cookware, the book includes mouth-watering recipes that put them to good use – several contributed by well-known chefs and food writers; the rest are my own.

I have not included every tool or piece of equipment, nor are all the items featured necessarily essential. The main criteria for inclusion were efficiency and comfort in use, durability in relation to cost and, finally, appearance. No matter how design-conscious a tool is, I find that function invariably wins out over style – in other words, if the shape of an item is determined by its use, it tends to be more credible than one that bows to the dictates of fashion. That said, I have included a few 'designer' items simply because they appeal. You will also find some ugly ducklings included for the same reason.

out which type of knife should be used for a particular job? Should the blade be straight or curved, rigid or flexible, long or short? Why do some frying pans have lids? Why do some pans have long handles and others short? Is stainless steel better than cast iron?

This book answers all these questions and many more. It provides essential information for evaluating and choosing new tools and cookware – whether it's a humble potato peeler or an expensive electric standing mixer. You'll find explanations of how tools work, if not obvious, and how to use them in the most efficient way. There is also a guide to the pros and cons of different materials and how to care for them. With this sort of information under your belt, you can make informed choices when you purchase equipment, and you will be able to cook with greater confidence and efficiency.

What you have in your kitchen is very much a personal choice, depending on how you live and what you like to cook. Build your 'batterie de cuisine' gradually, allowing it to evolve as your cooking style develops. I tend to use the same trusty old tools and pots and pans for years, but when my cooking changes in some way – perhaps as a result of foreign travel, or reading something inspiring, or discovering a new ingredient – I indulge in a new piece of equipment, and what a pleasure that is. It is always a joy to find a tool that makes preparation easier, or a pan that cooks more efficiently or one that is simply so pleasing that you never want to put it away.

Whether you are a novice or a proficient cook, I hope this book will inspire and inform, as well as open up the path to new and exciting culinary experiences.

material choice

This list explains briefly the pros and cons of the principal materials from which cooking equipment is made, and provides guidance on care and cleaning.

ALUMINIUM

Uses Pots, pans, bakeware, roasting pans, kettles, wrapping foil.
Pros Cheap, lightweight, conducts heat well and evenly as long as the gauge is heavy enough.
Cons Reacts with substances in food and therefore will discolour certain foods or impart a metallic taste. The metal itself tends to discolour and pit. Thin-gauge aluminium warps easily and heats unevenly.
Care Wash with hot soapy water, using a scouring pad if necessary. Remove stains by boiling in a weak solution of vinegar or cream of tartar.

ANODIZED ALUMINIUM

Uses As for aluminium.
Pros Anodizing is an electro-chemical process that gives aluminium a hard, dense oxide coating that resists corrosion. Hard-anodizing does not just produce a coating – it changes the molecular structure of aluminium, making it harder than steel while maintaining excellent heat distribution.
Cons Dishwasher detergents cause coloured anodized aluminium pans to fade.
Care Wash with hot, soapy water. Do not use scouring pads.

CAST IRON

Uses Pots, pans, griddles, grill pans, casseroles, baking dishes.
Pros Durable, strong, does not warp, conducts heat evenly and retains it well. Marvellous for long, slow cooking.
Cons Very heavy, so best for a pan that remains fairly static during cooking – e.g. a casserole. Its density makes it slow to heat. If dropped on a hard floor, it may break. If uncoated (with enamel or a non-stick surface), it needs seasoning with oil to prevent sticking and rusting.
Care Avoid washing uncoated cast iron; wipe with paper towels. Remove stuck-on food by lightly scouring under hot running water. Dry well and coat with oil before storing. Brush the cooking surface with oil before each use, then wipe off before adding oil for cooking. Wash coated cast iron with hot, soapy water but do not scour. To remove stubborn residue, leave the pan to soak for an hour or two.

COPPER

Uses Pots, pans, gratin dishes, roasting pans, egg bowls, moulds.
Pros The traditional choice of chefs as it is unbeaten for rapid and uniform heat conduction. Lasts for ever.
Cons Pricey and needs cosseting. If unlined, reacts with most foods, causing discolouration and mild toxicity if contact is prolonged. Unlined copper does not retain heat well. The traditional tin lining blisters or melts if overheated. Silver lining blackens on contact with the air and sulphurous compounds in some foods. Needs re-lining periodically.
Care Wash with hot, soapy water. Never use scouring pads. Soak to remove stuck-on food. Dry with soft cloth to bring up the shine. Use a proprietary cleaner for the outside, or rub with salt and vinegar or salt and lemon juice. Buff up the inside of silver-lined pans with a proprietary cleaner.

EARTHENWARE

Uses Casseroles, mixing bowls, gratin dishes, baking stones.
Pros Non-reactive, cheap, retains heat well and, as it is porous, moisture. Excellent for slow, moist cooking in the oven, or for use in a microwave oven.
Cons Dislikes sudden or extreme temperature changes. Not flameproof, but good-quality earthenware can be used on a heat diffuser over a low flame. Large rectangular and oval oven dishes are more prone to heat fracture than round ones.
Care Wash glazed, or partially glazed, pots with hot, soapy water without scouring. Completely unglazed pots such as a chicken brick or potato baker should be scrubbed clean with salty water. Don't use detergent as this will taint the food.

POLYTETRAFLUOROETHYLENE (non-stick coatings)

Trade names include Probon, Silverstone, Tefal, Teflon, Xylan.
Uses Pots, pans, roasting pans, grill pans, griddles, casseroles, bakeware, utensils.
Pros Modern non-stick coatings are tough and long-lasting.

Non-reactive and easy to clean, they are a boon for pans used for foods that stick, such as milk, and vital for low-fat cooking.
Cons The coating eventually wears off. Use utensils made of materials that are softer than the coating to prolong its life (e.g. wood, rubber or plastic). Not usually dishwasher-proof.
Care According to instructions. Avoid scouring and abrasive powders. Soak in warm water to remove stuck-on food.

PORCELAIN

Uses Soufflé dishes, ramekins, gratin dishes, tart pans.
Pros Looks fragile but can withstand heat so makes excellent oven-to-tableware. Retains heat and conducts it evenly. Can be used briefly under the grill. Non-porous and non-reactive.
Cons Extreme temperature changes will cause cracking. Needs heat-diffuser if used on the hob. Can be hard to clean.
Care Wash in hot, soapy water. Soak to remove stuck-on food. If scouring is needed use a plastic pad.

STAINLESS STEEL

Uses Pots, pans, roasting pans and racks, bowls, kettles, knives, utensils.
Pros Long-lasting and hygienic. Contains chrome, which is what makes it stainless, rustproof and non-reactive. Stainless-steel pots and pans also contain nickel. They may be described as 18/10, which means the ratio of chrome to nickel is 18% and 10% respectively. It is virtually immune to corrosion or pitting. Stainless steel used for most kitchen knives contains a lower level of chrome – at least 12% – and 0.15–0.80% carbon. Because of the reduction in chrome, it is more prone to staining, but the carbon provides strength.
Cons Poor and uneven conductor of heat. Manufacturers overcome this by giving pans a three- or five-layer sandwich base containing highly conductive metals such as aluminium or copper. Good stainless-steel pans have a base containing at least 5mm of aluminium or 3mm of copper. In the best-quality pans, the sandwiched layer continues up the sides, which prevents hot food from sizzling and sticking.
  Stainless steel is not entirely stainless – it will discolour, stain or spot if left in contact with hard water, salt water, lemon, vinegar or even some detergents if not rinsed and dried carefully after washing. Small pits may form.
Care Clean with hot, soapy water, using a nylon scourer if necessary. Avoid bleach or harsh abrasives. Soak burnt-on foods. Remove stubborn stains with a stainless-steel cleaner.

STONEWARE

Uses Casseroles, storage jars, bowls.
Pros Stronger than earthenware as it's fired at a higher temperature. Non-porous so does not need glazing. Ideal for dishes that need long, slow cooking in the oven.
Cons Does not take kindly to radical temperature changes.
Care As for glazed earthenware.

TEMPERED GLASS

Flameproof glass (Pyroflam), and ovenproof glass (Duralex, Pyrex)
Uses Flameproof: saucepans, casseroles, baking dishes. Ovenproof: casseroles, baking dishes, bowls, measuring jugs.
Pros Both types retain heat well, are non-reactive and are ideal for the microwave. Flameproof glass can be used on the hob and in the oven, and can be taken from freezer to oven.
Cons Flameproof glass is expensive. It conducts heat unevenly, so develops hot spots when used on the hob, causing food to stick. Ovenproof glass may crack at extreme temperature changes. It must be used with a heat diffuser on the hob.
Care Soak in hot soapy water to remove burnt-on food. Avoid metal scourers or harsh abrasives.

TITANIUM

Uses Casseroles, frying pans, sauté pans, grill pans.
Pros A rock-hard, light-weight metal that is naturally non-stick and virtually corrosion-resistant. It is great for low-fat cooking – the food sizzles round the pan with no oil. You can use metal utensils without causing damage.
Cons Expensive. Cannot be used on induction hobs.
Care Wash with warm, soapy water; do not scour.

VITREOUS ENAMEL

Uses Pots, pans, casseroles, pie dishes, bowls, roasting pans.
Pros Used to coat cast iron, aluminium or steel. Gives an easy-to-clean, non-porous coating that is taint- and scratch-proof.
Cons May chip if used with sharp-edged metal utensils.
Care Wash with hot, soapy water. Do not scrub with harsh abrasives. Leave to soak if necessary.

cutting peeling and piercing

basic blades

Next to your hands, the knife is probably the most important tool in the kitchen. If you buy good ones, use them with care and respect, and keep them in good condition, they should last your entire cooking life.

All knife blades are made of steel, which is why, traditionally, they have been manufactured in metal-working towns such as Solingen in Germany and Sheffield in England. The composition of steel varies, the amount of carbon present determining the blade's ability to hold its edge. Traditional carbon-steel blades are sharper but the metal stains and corrodes so other agents must be added. 'Stainless' steel contains chromium, which is rustproof but also more difficult to sharpen. Today, good-quality knives are made of high-carbon, no-stain steel, which is not quite stainless. Despite the carbon element, these knives neither rust nor corrode.

Blades are either forged or stamped, and the difference in quality is obvious. Forged blades are evenly balanced and beautifully tapered at the cutting edge, which results in greater flexibility. A stamped-bladed knife is thin and flat, and feels handle-heavy. You'll need to grip it more tightly and exert more pressure towards the front to compensate.

1 Bread knife The long, serrated blade cuts through bread or any other softish food with a tough crust or skin. Don't use serrated blades for cutting meat or dense-fleshed fruit and vegetables – you'll end up with a jagged mess.

2 Cook's knife The undisputed workhorse of the kitchen, the cook's knife has a characteristically wide blade and a graceful curve along the entire length of the cutting edge – designed to cope with repeated impact against a chopping board. Use it for chopping or dicing anything from hefty lumps of meat to the finest of herbs. Cook's knives come in a variety of lengths; a 20–25cm blade is the most useful for the home.

3 Utility knife As its name suggests, this knife can be used for a variety of cutting jobs, including slicing, peeling, paring and, depending on the length of the blade, carving. Although it is not designed for impact (the blade is narrower and less curved than the cook's knife), it can cope with chopping small amounts of not-too-tough food such as mushrooms or prawns. Look for a knife with a 13–18cm blade.

4 Tomato/sandwich knife Invaluable for tasks for which a bread knife would be too big. The serrated edge is useful for slicing food with a tough exterior and a soft centre, such as salami.

5 Paring knife Basically a miniature version of the cook's knife, a paring knife is used for peeling, scraping and slicing small fruits and vegetables. It is perhaps easier to use than a cook's knife when finely chopping garlic and ginger. The blade must be short – about 8–10cm.

6 Vegetable knife With its slightly upturned tip and short, curved blade, this knife comes in handy for peeling small, round vegetables, and for gouging eyes from potatoes and seeds from courgettes.

7 Knife block Instead of the usual slots, which can be fiddly, this block has tightly packed nylon filaments that hold knives without scratching them.

Choosing knives

Choose knives individually – don't be tempted to buy sets. Hold a knife to assess it. It should feel heavy for its size and evenly weighted, neither front- nor back-heavy. Do not be put off by weight – a heavy knife is more effective than a light one, and requires less effort to use.

The handle of the knife should be comfortable to hold. If it has rivets, the tops should be smooth and flush. Make sure the bolster (see 'Knife speak', page 12) fuses smoothly with the handle.

Each knife is designed for a specific purpose, so think about the types of food you regularly prepare before making a choice. Ideally, you should try to use the correct knife for the job. If funds are short, though, opt for the best quality and have fewer knives. It is possible to manage with one decent cook's knife and a paring knife. However, the six basic knives shown will give you more scope.

Knife care

Store your knives in a knife block so the blades are protected and the knives are easily accessible. A wall-mounted magnetic rack is another option, though some people question the safety of these (see 'Knife safety', page 12). Don't store knives loose in a drawer, as the cutting edges can be damaged by impact with other knives and utensils.

Damage will be caused, too, by dumping knives in the washing-up bowl. Some of the better-quality knives are dishwasher-proof, but if yours are not, wash, rinse and dry them individually immediately after use. Don't leave knives to soak.

To keep your knives in prime condition, give each one a few strokes on a steel whenever you use it. Fast, flamboyant sharpening is not essential. More important is maintaining a 20° angle and sharpening the full length of the blade (see 'Using a steel', above). Treat the blade with care by using a wooden or polyethylene board to chop on. Don't use a plate or the work surface, as hard materials such as glass, granite or metal will harm the cutting edge.

Using a steel: method 1 Hold the steel vertically on a firm surface. Grasp the knife low on the handle, with the blade at a 20° angle to the steel. Bring the knife down and across the steel, drawing it to you so the tip meets the steel at the base. Reverse the action, holding the other side of the blade against the other side of the steel and pushing away from you. Repeat both actions until the blade is sharp.

Using a steel: method 2 Grasp the steel in one hand and the knife in the other. Place the handle ends of each together, with the blade at a 20° angle to the steel. Raise the elbows and part your hands so the blade travels up the steel, finishing with the tip of the blade against the steel. Repeat, holding the other side of the blade against the other side of the steel. Repeat both movements until the blade is sharp.

8 V-shaped sharpener The outer casing houses cunningly arranged, crossed pairs of steel rods set on springs and positioned at the 20° sharpening angle. The rods mimic the action of a conventional steel as the blade is drawn across them. This is a good tool for those who have difficulty using a steel.

9 Carborundum stone Carborundum is the trade name for a group of rock-hard abrasives, usually composed of silicon carbide. The stones are useful for smoothing out small scratches or indentations. The best ones have two grades of surface: fairly fine on one side and coarser on the other. Most stones are rectangular in shape, though the one shown here resembles a dumpy steel. To use a stone, first lubricate it with water or cooking oil. Holding the knife blade at a 15–20° angle to the stone, pass the length of the blade over the stone. Turn the knife over and repeat in the opposite direction. Repeat both movements several times until the blade is sharp.

10 Sharpening steel Somewhat surprisingly, a steel works not by sharpening, but by realigning the molecules that form the cutting edge. They are knocked out of alignment by repeated chopping.

A steel needs to be made of a substance that is harder than the tool to be sharpened. Ceramic or diamond-coated steels are hardest of all. Traditional steels are cylindrical with grooves running along the length of the rod, but some are oval or flat and others still have smoother surfaces. The finer the surface, the keener will be the finish. Choose a steel with a shaft that is longer than the blade of your biggest knife.

This superb steel is diamond-coated and has a flat, relatively smooth surface, providing greater contact than a cylindrical steel.

8

9

10

beyond basics

As you become more experienced, you will undoubtedly want to add to your knife collection. The knives shown here are for specialist tasks or for dealing with specific foods. Some of them are expensive, but good knives are good to have, and once you've got them you can easily justify their existence. Buy oysters, eat grapefruit, or fillet your own fish....

Knife speak

O **Butt** The downward-curving tip of the handle. This cushions your hand against the impact of chopping.

O **Handle** The part attached to the tang. Make sure it feels comfortable and is neither too large nor too small for you to grip firmly.

O **Tang** The unsharpened part of the knife blade that extends into the handle. The longer the tang, the better balanced will be the knife.

O **Bolster** The splayed metal section on a forged blade that butts up flush to the handle. The bolster strengthens the blade and keeps your hand away from the cutting area.

O **Blade** The flattish part of the knife that forms the cutting edge.

Knife safety
Knives are dangerous tools. That said, if they are treated with respect rather than with presumption, they will be less likely to cause accidents.

O *Never* test for sharpness by running your finger along the cutting edge. If you cannot resist touching the blade, brush your finger lightly *across* it.

O A sharp knife is safer than a blunt one. A blunt knife needs more pressure to cut and could slip.

O If you use a magnetic rack for storage, make sure it is out of reach of children and pets.

O Don't leave knives hidden under soapy water in the washing-up bowl.

O Don't use a knife with a greasy handle.

O If you leave a knife on the work surface, ensure that neither the handle nor blade protrude over the edge. The knife could easily be grabbed by a child or knocked onto the floor or, worse still, onto someone's foot.

1 Chopping boards Wood is the preferred material for most chopping, but is not recommended for raw poultry as it cannot be sterilized. It is attractive, easy to care for and least damaging to knife blades. Choose the sturdiest board you can find, preferably at least 4cm thick. This one has cleated ends to prevent warping and cracking.
Polyethylene boards, though less pleasing visually, have an advantage over wood in that they can be sterilized with bleach or boiling water – essential after preparing raw poultry. They are also dishwasher-proof. The rough-textured surface prevents both the food and the board from slipping, while a groove around the perimeter helps to stop any liquid from overflowing.

2 Carving knife and fork
A carving knife glides cleanly through meat as if it were butter, while the fork enables you to anchor the meat in place without piercing it. Choose a knife with a blade that is at least 20cm long. This one has a beautifully subtle taper along the back, creating a narrow tip for assiduous probing of meat and bone. The generous curve on the underside effectively extends the cutting edge. The fork has bayonet prongs, rather than the curved type that follow more closely the contours of the meat. Press the sides of the prongs firmly down on the meat to hold it while you carve.

3 Ham/smoked salmon slicer This is used for carving thin, elongated slices. The blade is narrow and reasonably flexible, and must be at least 25cm in length. It has a very slight taper through its thickness, enabling you to produce impressively straight slices, rather than veering diagonally off-course – an effect caused by a more pronounced taper.

4 Freezer knife A freezer knife is not wholeheartedly recommended, as food texture and appearance may suffer if you hack at it while still frozen – it is better to let food defrost before cutting. If you do buy one, a strong, deeply toothed blade is a must. The blade should be longer than the largest item you are likely to cut.

5 Filleting knife This elegant knife has a thin, gently curved blade, which is sufficiently pliable to remain in close contact with the contours of fish or poultry. The blade needs to be at least 18cm long, and should be kept scrupulously sharp in order to do its job.

6 Boning knife A boning knife has a tapered blade with a sharp point. Blades are flexible or rigid, and 1.5–2.5cm in width. A wide, rigid blade is good for a large cut of meat with simple bones, while a narrow, flexible blade copes with poultry or fish.

7 'Universal' cheese knife The blade of this knife has holes that prevent cheese from sticking to it, while the serrated cutting edge copes with hard cheese. The forked tip assists with transferring cheese to a plate.

8 Parmesan knife The rigid, leaf-shaped blade of this dumpy little knife prizes chunks from hard cheeses such as Parmesan. Embed it in the cheese and twist.

9 Grapefruit knife The long, thin, serrated blade, with a curved tip, neatly cuts between the pith and flesh, following the contours of the fruit.

10 Oyster knife Two short, arrow-shaped cutting edges prize open the shell, breaking its vacuum. The guard at the hilt protects the hand and also prevents the knife from thrusting into the shell and out the other side. The pointed tip is used to sever the oyster meat from the shell.

11 Cleaver Equally useful for demolishing bones or shredding spring onions, the blade of the cleaver is thick and rigid throughout most of its width, before tapering abruptly to a sharp bevel. The greater the weight, the less effort required, so buy the heaviest cleaver you can use with comfort. A 15cm blade is about the right length. This modern-style cleaver has a seamless blade and handle, which makes it easy to clean. Use the hole to hang your cleaver on the wall out of harm's way.

Japanese knives
12 Sometimes called a sashimi knife, the long yanagi is single-bevelled like the deba (see below). The blade glides through raw fish, producing immaculately straight, paper-thin slices for sushi. The knife is also used to slice and chop vegetables, and to produce intricate oriental garnishes.
13 Somewhat surprisingly, the medium-length, wide-bladed deba is used for the delicate task of boning and filleting fish. This is made possible by Japanese-style grinding, in which the blade is bevelled over a wide area on one side and the opposite side is left flat. This creates a razor-sharp, acutely angled cutting edge that slips effortlessly between flesh and bone.

Filleting flat fish

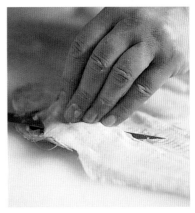

1 Place the fish on a chopping board. With the point of a filleting knife, cut the fish to the bone behind the gills, across the tail and round the edge of the flesh. This defines the shape of the fillets. Slice along the backbone from head to tail, down to the bone.

2 Holding the knife almost flat, slide it under the flesh, beginning at the backbone. Keeping the knife flat, use a gentle sawing motion to ease away the first fillet from the bones. Repeat on the other side of the backbone for the second fillet.

3 Turn the fish over. Use the knife point to define the shape of the third and fourth fillets, and cut down the backbone as described in step 1. Ease the fillets gently away from the bones as described in step 2.

Boning a whole chicken breast

1 Place skin-side down on a polyethylene chopping board. Grip the breast at either end and twist backwards to separate the breast- and collarbones. Poke your fingers into the flesh to locate the wishbone and remove it with the tip of a boning knife.

2 With the skin-side facing down, use a gentle scraping motion with the tip end of the blade to carefully cut away the flesh from either side of the breastbone. Once the flesh is cut free, remove the breastbone.

3 Cut the flesh away from the ribs, following the contours of the bones and cutting as close to them as possible. Remove the ribs and cut out the remaining cartilage. Trim the breasts neatly according to your chosen recipe.

Carving a leg of lamb

1 Place the meat on a carving board with the meatier side uppermost. Wrap the shank end in a napkin. Carve thin slices from the rounded side of the leg, cutting away from you and almost parallel with the bone.

2 Turn the leg over and carve about the same number of slices from the opposite side, slicing along the length of the leg and almost parallel with the bone.

3 Insert the carving knife at the shank end of the leg and carve small, thin slices of meat from the bone. Try to carve an equal number of slices from each part of the leg.

Hong Kong-style broccoli and baby corn

Contributed by Ken Hom, a leading authority on Asian cooking, this easy-to-prepare stir-fry puts the cleaver to good use. As Ken says, 'Once you gain facility with a cleaver, you will see how it can be used on all types of food to slice, dice, chop, fillet, shred, crush or whatever'.

Serves 4–6 as a side dish or light meal

Tools	Ingredients
preparation bowls	50g Chinese dried black mushrooms
	450g broccoli
strainer	225g baby corn
cleaver	1 tsp salt
vegetable peeler	½ tsp freshly ground black pepper
	1 tsp sugar
large saucepan	1 tbsp Shaoxing rice wine or pale dry sherry
wok or large frying pan	1 tbsp light soy sauce
wok ladle or long-handled wooden spoon	3 tbsp oyster sauce or dark soy sauce
	1½ tbsp groundnut oil
	2 tsp dark sesame oil

1 Soak the black mushrooms in warm water for 20 minutes. Drain them and squeeze out the excess liquid. Remove and discard the stems and finely shred the caps into thin strips. Set aside.

2 Separate the broccoli heads into small florets, then peel and slice the stems. Blanch the broccoli pieces and baby corn in a large pot of boiling salted water for 3 minutes, then immerse them in cold water. Drain thoroughly.

3 Combine the salt, pepper, sugar, rice wine, soy sauce and oyster sauce in a small bowl.

4 Heat a wok or large frying pan over high heat. Add the groundnut oil and when it is very hot and slightly smoking, add the broccoli, corn and mushrooms. Stir-fry for 3 minutes.

5 Add the seasoning and sauce mixture and continue stir-frying at a moderate-to-high heat for 2 minutes, until the vegetables are heated through.

6 Add the sesame oil and stir-fry for another 30 seconds. The vegetables are ready to serve.

Using a cleaver Hold the food with your fingertips curled under so your middle knuckles act as a guide for the blade. Don't raise the cleaver higher than your knuckles. Position the blade about 3mm from the edge of the food and slice downwards. Control the thickness of the slices by moving your fingers either away from or towards the edge being cut. To slice diagonally, position your fingers at a slant and use this to guide the blade.

more cutting tools

These tools are designed to ease fiddly or time-consuming food preparation tasks, such as slicing, chopping, shredding and peeling. The end result is usually neater than it would be if you had not used the tool. These are not mere gadgets; they've all been around for years and have proved their worth.

Vegetable peelers

1 Practical and economical, the all-metal swivel peeler has a central slot that is wide and long enough not to trap peelings. The slot is sharpened on both sides, so it suits both left- and right-handed users. The swivel action enables the tool to follow more accurately the contours of the item being peeled, reducing wastage.

2 Instantly recognizable by its string-wrapped handle, this traditional British peeler has a V-shaped blade with a narrow slot, which can become clogged. The sharpened tip digs out blemishes.

3 This smart Y-shaped peeler was originally designed for the manually disabled. It has a swivel blade and the handle is made of a non-slip rubber and polypropylene composite. The extra thickness makes it easier to grip.

4 Canelle knife or lemon stripper A protruding, V-shaped tooth gouges out thin lengths of peel from citrus fruits. The knife can also be used to cut narrow grooves from unpeeled cucumbers or mushrooms, creating a scalloped edge when the vegetables are sliced. The tool shown is for right-handed use only, though left-handed models are available.

5 Citrus zester Five sharp-edged holes set into an angled blade tip produce flavoursome wisps of citrus zest to use for decorating cakes and desserts. The blade's shallow angle ensures that it cuts only into the zest, or outer surface of the peel, rather than into the bitter pith.

6 Pizza wheel When it comes to dividing up pizza, the pizza wheel outclasses even the sharpest knife. The wobble-free, circular blade carves cleanly through topping and crust, giving neat, manageable slices. The guard protects your fingers from slipping onto the blade.

7 Cheese plane This efficient tool was originally designed for shaving wafer-thin slices from Scandinavian cheeses too pungent to be eaten in larger amounts. The angled cutting edge guides slices through a slot and onto the spade-shaped blade. The blade supports the cheese and stops it from splitting as it is transported to your plate.

Bean slicers

8 The small plastic slicer works like magic on runner beans, simultaneously removing the strings and slicing the bean into spaghetti-like strands. Simply insert a bean into the hole and push it through the four blades. When it emerges, grasp the end and pull. Beans need to be crisp and firm, and the tool is practical for small amounts only.

9 This sturdy, cast-iron slicer is useful for processing large quantities of any type of bean. Beans are fed through slots into the path of three very sharp blades set into a disc that revolves as you turn the crank handle. They emerge as paper-thin, diagonally cut slices with no evidence of stringiness. One possible drawback is that the clamp cannot be attached to a work surface that is thicker than 3cm.

10 Hard-boiled egg slicer Ten taut wires attached to a frame cut cleanly and evenly through white and yolk. Since the wires do not drag, the yolk does not crumble.

Mandolin

11 The stainless steel and black fibreglass model zips through vegetables with the utmost precision. Depending on the shape and position of the blade, you can quickly cut any firm vegetable into slices, matchsticks, waffles or ripples. Just hold the piece of vegetable firmly and pass it across the blades. There are alternative blades, and an adjustable gauge determines thickness of cut. Rubber feet hold it safely in place, and a guard protects your fingers. However, it is expensive.

12 Much cheaper, but altogether cruder, is the wooden mandolin. Though it has drawbacks – namely a tendency to warp, and a lack of supporting feet – it is a classic and, unless you want one hundred per cent precision, it does the job perfectly well.

13 Mezzaluna Used mainly for cutting herbs, the mezzaluna ('half-moon' in Italian) works on the same principle as a cook's knife – a curved blade rocks back and forth over the material to be chopped. The two handles enable you to exert an even downward pressure, while the crescent-shaped blade increases the length of the cutting edge. Some types have two or even three blades. Though this speeds up chopping, more time needs to be spent scraping herbs from the blades.

14 Hachoir The half-moon cutting blade and identically shaped bowl are ideal for chopping ginger, garlic or small amounts of herbs.

15 Chip cutter This is the tool for those who prefer regimented chips to homely hand-cut ones. Push down the handle to force a peeled potato through a cutting grid. Alternative grids provide a choice of chip sizes, ranging from fat to thin.

16 Fish tweezers These tweezers alleviate the anxiety that sometimes accompanies eating fish. The 15.5cm shafts terminate in rounded tips that are ridged on the inner sides. When clamped together, there is enough surface area to grasp and tweeze out lurking bones.

17 Fish scaler The underside of this solid aluminium tool is covered with close-set, sharp-edged studs that catch on the scales, lifting and ripping them out as you pass the scaler over the fish. If possible, descale your fish before gutting it – the fish will be firmer and rounder, and therefore easier to manipulate.

cutting, peeling and piercing **17**

Cutting vegetables

Vegetables cut into pieces of a uniform shape and size cook more evenly and improve the appearance of the finished dish. Most vegetables need to be cut in a particular way to suit the cooking method. With its wide, rigid blade, and gently curved cutting edge, the cook's knife is the best one to use for chopping, slicing and dicing. A vegetable knife is better for peeling and slicing small vegetables and for gouging the eyes from potatoes. When cutting vegetables, always use a chopping board to protect your knife blades.

Chopping onions Peel the onion, leaving the root on, then slice in half from top to bottom with a cook's knife. Lay each half cut-side down on a chopping board. Slice thinly lengthways, stopping short at the root (to hold the slices together), then slice thinly crossways. Discard the piece with the root. This method causes fewer tears than haphazard chopping – as the onion is held together during chopping, tear-inducing chemicals have less chance of escaping.

Slicing Chinese cabbage Remove any damaged outer leaves, then use a cook's knife to quarter or halve the cabbage from top to bottom. Place cut-side down and slice diagonally, beginning from the stalk end. Angled slices not only look attractive, they also increase the area of cut edges exposed to the fat or liquid, thus reducing the time needed for cooking.

Dicing celery Using a cook's knife, trim the root and leaves from the stems. Remove any tough strings with a swivel peeler. Lay the stems on a board and slice them lengthways into three or four pieces of even width. Slice the wide part of the stems near the root into shorter strips that are the same width as the other pieces. Lay all the strips flat and slice crossways to produce small squares.

Julienning carrots Use a vegetable knife or cook's knife to trim the carrots. Peel with a vegetable knife or peeler. With a cook's knife, slice a thin strip off one side so the carrot lies flat. Slice crossways into 5cm pieces. Cut these lengthways into vertical slices about as thin as a matchstick. Stack the slices and slice again into thin strips, keeping the tip of the knife on the board as you rock the blade to and fro.

Cutting round vegetables into segments Depending on the vegetable's size, use a cook's knife or a vegetable knife. If cutting tomatoes, as shown here, use a very sharp vegetable knife or a serrated knife. Slice the vegetable in half from top to bottom. Place the halves cut-side down on a chopping board and slice in half again. Slice each quarter.

Ribbon-cutting leafy vegetables To make the leaves easier to roll, remove any thick stems by cutting through the ribs with a cook's knife, close to either side of the stem. If the leaves are very wide, cut them in half lengthways. Stack the leaves and roll them into a tight wad. Slice the roll crossways into strips of the required width.

summer squash salad

The recipe for this colourful summer salad was contributed by Anne Willan, founder of the famous La Varenne cookery school at Château du Feÿ in Burgundy, France, and one of the world's most trusted teachers. Her favourite tool is a black Matfer mandolin, which zips through the squash, cutting them into thin julienne sticks. The salad can be served at once, or after an hour or so, when the vegetables have wilted and softened slightly, though remaining crisp.

Serves 6–8 as a starter

Tools	Ingredients
cook's knife	4 small green courgettes, weighing about 450g
mandolin	4 small yellow courgettes or other yellow squash, weighing about 450g
bowl	juice of 2 lemons or limes
citrus juicer	2 shallots, finely chopped
small flat whisk	salt and freshly ground black pepper
	125ml vegetable oil, such as grapeseed or sunflower
	2 tbsp chopped fresh dill (or your favourite fresh herb)
	fresh dill or other herb sprigs, to garnish

1 Trim the ends from the courgettes and cut them into 5cm lengths.
2 Slice the pieces of courgette lengthways on the julienne blade of a mandolin (a), rotating them as you slice, so that you come up with a julienne of the colourful outer peel and some of the flesh, but discarding the seeds and central core. Tip into a bowl.
3 Make a vinaigrette dressing by whisking the lemon or lime juice with the shallots, salt and pepper. Then whisk in the oil and add the herbs.
4 Toss the vegetable julienne with the dressing, taste, and adjust the seasoning. Divide between individual serving plates and garnish with a small sprig of dill or your chosen herb.

With its two handles and gentle rocking motion, the mezzaluna creates an even downward pressure that speedily reduces a mountain of fresh herbs to a mound, cutting cleanly through the leaves without bruising them.

pasta with fresh herbs, lemon zest and broad beans

Requiring a range of cutting tools, this recipe combines fragrant herbs such as thyme, savory and oregano with a generous amount of lemon zest to produce a bright, fresh-flavoured dish. Savory goes particularly well with broad beans, and the toasted breadcrumbs add a pleasing crunch. Prepare the herbs, lemon zest and Parmesan shavings just before you start to cook.

Serves 4

Tools	Ingredients
mezzaluna	250g dried flat, long pasta such as linguine or fettuccine
small cook's knife	
chopping board	200g podded baby broad beans, fresh or frozen
citrus zester	
swivel peeler	8 tbsp olive oil
small roasting pan for toasting breadcrumbs	1 garlic clove, thinly sliced
	1 small bunch flat-leaf parsley, finely chopped
pasta pot	good handful mixed fresh herbs such as fresh basil, oregano, thyme or savory, finely chopped
medium-sized frying pan	
	finely shredded zest of 1 1/2 lemons
	4 tbsp stale breadcrumbs, toasted in the oven
	sea salt flakes
	coarsely ground black pepper
	fresh Parmesan shavings, to garnish

Using a mezzaluna Working from one end to the other, and using a rocking motion, chop the sprigs crossways into very thin shreds about 2–3mm wide. For even thinner shreds, turn the mezzaluna and chop in the opposite direction.

Using a citrus zester To cut away the outer layer of lemon zest without removing the bitter pith, drag the zester across the peel, exerting firm pressure to produce thin, short shreds. Cutting longer shreds needs more practice.

To make Parmesan shavings Hold a lump of Parmesan in one hand and a swivel peeler in the other. Drag the peeler over the surface to shave away thin wafers.

1 Cook the pasta in plenty of boiling, salted water until 'al dente' – tender but still with some bite. Drain thoroughly and tip into a warmed serving dish.

2 Meanwhile, plunge the beans into a pan of boiling water. Bring back to the boil, boil for 1 minute, then drain.

3 Heat the oil in a frying pan until it is very hot but not smoking. Toss in the garlic, cook for a few seconds, then remove the pan from the heat the moment the garlic starts to colour. Immediately stir in the herbs and lemon zest.

4 Toss the entire contents of the pan over the pasta. Add a generous seasoning of sea salt and black pepper, and toss thoroughly to mix. Now add the beans and breadcrumbs. Toss again briefly – don't let the beans disappear to the bottom of the dish – and scatter over a few Parmesan shavings.

the art of chopping herbs

Preparing herbs for chopping
Trim off the coarse stalks immediately below the lower leaves. Place the sprigs on a chopping board, facing in the same direction with the stalk ends lining up.

The way fresh herbs are prepared has a direct bearing on the appearance and flavour of the finished dish. Once torn or cut, their delicate leaves release volatile oils into the atmosphere or into the surrounding food or liquid. Cutting too soon or too much can reduce a fragrant bunch of fresh, green herbs to a dismal pile of bruised shreds.

The secret of cutting herbs is to use a razor-sharp tool and to make as few cuts as possible. You can still chop your herbs finely, if that is what you want, but it must be done in a controlled and orderly way, instead of hacking them haphazardly.

For example, to prepare leafy, stemmy herbs such as parsley, coriander and mint, first nip off the coarse stalks immediately below the last usable pair of leaves. Do this before you wash them because dry herbs are easier to handle than wet. If you're sure your herbs are uncontaminated and they are not too dusty, don't worry about washing them. Otherwise, dunk them briefly in cold water, drain and dry them well in a salad spinner and then on paper towels. If you're going to use the stalks to flavour a stock, they will obviously have to be washed too.

Next place your herbs on a chopping board, facing in the same direction with the stalk ends lined up. If you have an untidy heap, you'll need to make more cuts than necessary and the job will take longer. Now chop in one direction, as thinly as possible, working from one end of the bunch to the other. If you want the herbs finer, chop in the opposite direction and work down the bunch again; finer still – chop at an angle. This way you will have cut in only two or three directions and your herbs stand a chance of retaining their identity.

The choice of tool is whatever you feel most comfortable with. Some cooks are wedded to a mezzaluna, others swear by a cook's knife. Food processors are generally not recommended as the blade is never as sharp as that of a good hand tool and they therefore do not cut so cleanly. The high speed of the processor's blade also causes bruising.

Whether using a knife or a mezzaluna, a regular and controlled rocking motion is needed. The mezzaluna creates an even pressure and is less laborious to use. To chop herbs with a cook's knife, bunch them tightly with your free hand a couple of centimetres from the top end of the bunch, curling your fingertips inwards. Place the blade across the pile and slice very thinly, using your knuckle as a guide for the blade. Then move your free hand down and cut another section. Another method is to hold down the knife tip with one hand and rock the blade across the pile, using the tip as a pivot.

Small quantities of tender herbs or young rosemary shoots can simply be snipped with scissors, either directly over the finished dish or into a container.

tools for shearing and piercing

Scissors and shears cut cleanly, leaving no jagged edges. Many people prefer to use scissors instead of a knife, as more muscular control can be exercised when cutting, and fingers are kept safely out of the way of the blades. A strong pair of kitchen scissors can be used for a range of tasks, such as cutting paper and string, trimming fins from fish and tips from artichokes, snipping herbs and bacon rind, and cutting dried fruit into bite-size chunks. If they are sturdy enough, kitchen scissors will even sever poultry, though poultry shears make lighter work of it.

There are numerous occasions when food or certain types of container need to be pierced, and there are a variety of tools designed to do the job. Basic piercing tools such as skewers and corkscrews are essential kitchen kit. However, some tools are so specialist they border on mirth-provoking; others still are so flimsily made they aren't worth kitchen drawer space. But there are surprises – you'll often find you get attached to a tool and it becomes indispensable.

1 Kitchen shears The blades of these neat, all-purpose shears have a notch for cutting through poultry joints, while various parts of the handle can be used for opening jars and bottles, prizing off lids, and as a screwdriver. The shears can be taken apart for washing and are dishwasher proof.
2 Kitchen scissors These differ from household scissors in having longer blades, and one is usually serrated, making it easier to cut chicken or fish. The best scissors have forged blades and are made of stainless steel, which will not rust. Choose a pair with a screw rather than a rivet, so you can take the blades apart for cleaning or sharpening. Check handles for comfort.
3 Poultry shears These shears easily sever bones, sinew and flesh. The blades are curved and pointed for intricate cutting, and a notch holds bones firmly during cracking. The strong spring kicks the handles apart, but it is a trap for raw poultry juices and needs thorough cleaning after use. A hook holds the handles together during storage.

Corers
To use a corer, push the circular cutting edge vertically through the middle of a fruit or vegetable, then withdraw it, bringing the core out in the cylinder. If you veer from the vertical, remnants of pip and core will be left embedded in the flesh, as they will if the core's diameter is greater than the cylinder's.
4 The shorter apple corer works reasonably well on apples and pears but is not suitable for anything longer.
5 To core courgettes, aubergines and other elongated vegetables, you will need the longer vegetable corer.

6 Pineapple corer/slicer This tool does work, but it is probably worth buying only if you eat pineapples on a regular basis. Slice the top off the pineapple, then wind the slicer down over the core. When it reaches the bottom, pull upwards and out will come a continuous spiral of pineapple flesh, devoid of unwelcome brown spots. The shell remains intact, ready for retro dishes such as pineapple boats.

7 Melon baller The melon baller is useful for occasions when neat spheres of melon are preferable to rough-cut chunks. To use the baller, press it deep into the flesh until juice flows from the hole in the base of the bowl. Then twist and remove. Some ballers have a smaller scoop at the other end, for removing shallow flesh close to the rind.

8 Cherry pitter There are times when the effort of pitting cherries is either worth it or necessary: for example, when making a cherry pie, when bottling and pickling cherries, or when feeding the very young. Though still laborious, the process is speeded up by a pitter, which also does the job neatly.

Load the cherries into the sloping tray, where they are funnelled one by one into a stoning cradle. When you work the plunger, a metal rod pierces the fruit and removes the stone. The stone drops into the plastic container and the fruit falls into a bowl placed in front of the pitter. The tool also works reasonably well on olives.

Skewers

Skewers conduct heat through food, close flaps and hold things in place. They are also used for testing cakes and poultry for doneness, and for piercing small citrus fruits and the skin of fatty birds to allow juice or fat to flow during cooking.

9 Bamboo skewers do not conduct heat as well as metal ones, but they are fine for small kebabs such as chicken satay. Though some cooks advise soaking bamboo skewers in water before use, I never do, and so far have not had to deal with a serious conflagration.

10 Kebab skewers are made of flat metal to prevent impaled food from spinning round when you turn the skewer over. The most useful size is 25–30cm, though there are longer and more flamboyant models for gaucho-style barbecues. Stainless-steel skewers are rustproof and easiest to keep clean.

11 Small round skewers, sometimes called poultry lacers, come in a range of sizes and are ideal for sealing poultry orifices and closing flaps. String can be threaded through the eye and used to close cavities more securely. The skewers are also useful for securing small parcels of food. Butcher's skewers are used in much the same way.

12 Potato baking spike Four metal spikes speed up baking by conducting heat to the centre of the potato. There are drawbacks: baked-on starch is very difficult to remove from the spikes, the tool takes up a fair amount of oven space, and if you cook less than four potatoes it becomes unbalanced. The spike is worth having, however, if you regularly bake potatoes for four people.

Can openers

A good can opener should work cleanly and continuously without coming to a halt halfway round the can. It should be effortless to use and feel comfortable in the hand.

13 The blue opener is easy to operate and is suitable for both right- and left-handed people. It is marginally less safe than some types, though, as it removes the entire rim of the can, leaving a clean but exposed sharp edge.

14 The chrome opener has an easy-to-grip butterfly handle and rounded black plastic inserts that protect the palms. The steel blade hooks over the rim of the can, leaving it in place once cutting is complete.

Corkscrews

Being a firm believer in 'cook's nips', I see the corkscrew as an essential tool. Even if you rarely imbibe, you will need wine for sauces and gravies.

15 This screw-pull corkscrew has a comfortable handle and an 'endless', Teflon®-coated, spiral shaft that turns until the cork emerges. The shaft is open, with a well-rounded profile, enabling it to grip corks firmly (solid-shafted spirals do not grip as well).

16 Easy to use and reliable, this winged, stainless steel corkscrew has a self-centring frame that sits on the bottle rim, guiding the solid-shafted spiral through the cork. Turn the handle until the wings are fully raised, then press them down to remove the cork.

17 This state-of-the-art, lever-based model may look fearsome, but it's easy to use. With the lever fully open and the pincers gripping the bottle, swing the lever up and over to the closed position. This drives the screw into the cork. Swing the lever back to the open position and the cork will emerge.

18 'Universal' opener Not strictly for piercing, this tool forces open unwilling lids and can cope with several sizes. Serrated inner edges create enough traction to grip and loosen the lid as you twist, while the sturdy non-slip handles allow you to use plenty of force. Various protuberances act as vacuum releasers, crown cap removers and can piercers. The tool saves time, reduces frustration and more than justifies its existence.

spatchcocked poussins
with rosemary-and-orange butter

The best way to grill whole birds is to cut out the backbone with poultry shears and press the carcass flat. They form a neat, flat shape that cooks evenly and quickly. Skewers keep the birds rigid when you turn them and help to conduct heat through to the thickest part of the thigh. Pushing herb butter under the skin keeps the flesh deliciously juicy.

Serves 4

Tools	Ingredients
mezzaluna or cook's knife	100g unsalted butter, softened to room temperature
garlic press	2 tbsp finely chopped rosemary
citrus grater	1 large garlic clove, crushed
pestle and mortar	finely grated zest of 1 small orange
small bowl	1/2 tsp black peppercorns, crushed
fork	generous pinch of sea salt flakes
polyethylene chopping board	2 poussins, each weighing about 450g
poultry shears or strong kitchen scissors	a few small rosemary sprigs, to garnish
4 flat metal skewers	
grill pan with rack	

1 Combine the butter, rosemary, garlic, orange zest, peppercorns and sea salt flakes, mixing well with a fork.

2 Put the birds on a polyethylene board, breast-side down. Using poultry shears or strong kitchen scissors, cut off the wing tips and lumpy joints at the end of the legs. Remove the backbone and parson's nose by cutting along the entire length of the bird, either side of the backbone (a).

3 Open out the birds and turn them breast-side up. Press down sharply with the heel of your hand to break and flatten the breastbone (b).

4 Separate the skin from the meat on the breasts, thighs and drumsticks by carefully inserting your fingers between the skin and the flesh. Push knobs of the seasoned butter under the skin, spreading it as evenly as possible and moulding it to the shape of the birds (c). Cover and leave in the fridge for at least 2 hours, or up to 24 hours.

5 When ready to grill, arrange the flattened birds so the drumsticks are turned inwards, nestling close to the rib cage. Insert a metal skewer diagonally through the thigh, drumstick and breast on one side and out through the wing on the other side (d). Insert a second skewer in the same way from the opposite side.

6 Heat the grill until very hot. Place the poussins breast-side down on a rack in a clean grill pan and position the pan 15cm from the heat source. Grill for 15 minutes, then turn over and grill for another 15 minutes, or until the juices are no longer pink when you pierce the thickest part of the thigh.

7 Pull out the skewers – use oven gloves as they will be hot. Using clean poultry shears or kitchen scissors, cut each poussin into quarters, and pile up in a warmed serving dish. Pour the buttery juices over, scraping up the sticky, tasty sediment from the bottom of the pan. Garnish with a sprig or two of rosemary and serve at once.

electric mixers and processors

These multi-purpose machines not only chop and slice, but shred, beat, juice, whisk and mix. They work at high speed, and are ideal for processing large quantities of ingredients quickly.

Although they are convenient, these items deprive cooks of some of the pleasure of preparing food. They also make it difficult to detect subtle physical changes in food while it is being processed. If you become reliant on a machine before you have learnt to perform the tasks manually, you are unlikely to develop a true understanding of how and why ingredients behave as they do. That said, electric mixers and processors are worth their weight in gold if used judiciously. Having made the financial outlay, make sure your mixer or processor earns its keep. You are more likely to use a machine if it is permanently within reach on the work surface, rather than hidden in a cupboard.

I Standing mixer A classic mixer for the serious home baker, this machine has a 4 litre stainless-steel bowl that holds 2.25kg of ingredients. The rotary head 'moves like Elvis', gyrating from the inside to the outside of the bowl in a series of circles, drawing in every scrap of mixture from the sides and base, and mixing it quickly, evenly and thoroughly. The mixer has three basic attachments – a wire whip, a flat beater and a dough hook – as well as numerous optional extras for a wide variety of tasks.

2 Food processor The food processor has become a near-necessity in the modern kitchen. The S-shaped blade effectively chops meat, vegetables and fruit; makes breadcrumbs; mixes dough; purées soups; and whisks dressings. Alternative cutting discs can be fitted to grate, shred and slice.

Choose a processor with the largest container you can find. If the container sits on top of the motor, make sure it is not too tall to fit between the work surface and high-level cupboards. If space is tight, choose a processor with the container set next to the motor.

Though it is useful, the processor is not without drawbacks. Pieces of food tend to get stuck between the grating disk and the lid. It is not recommended for chopping herbs, and cannot be used for processing small quantities of food. If the mixture is not sufficiently liquid, the sides of the container will need to be continually scraped down.

3 Stick blender Even lighter and more compact than a hand-held mixer, a stick blender is useful for blending small portions of food and frothing up liquids – though for some tasks a whisk would be just as good.

This model is sold with a useful mixing beaker, the diameter of which is slightly larger than that of the blades. This means that even a very small amount of food will come above the top of the blades, so it is ideal for making baby food. A whisk and a chopping attachment are also supplied.

4 Blender A kitchen classic, this deco blender has a powerful two-speed motor and a large, heat-resistant goblet. It blends, mixes and juices, whizzing up the smoothest of smoothies, velvety sauces, soups, purées and crushed ice. With its small diameter, the goblet keeps food within reach of the short, straight blades, so you don't have to keep stopping and stirring. Though a blender copes with smaller amounts of food than a processor, there must be enough to cover the blades. You will also need to add liquid, otherwise the food at the top will not be blended.

5 Juicer This machine transforms fruit and vegetables into pulp-free, health-promoting juice. Peeled fruit or vegetables are pushed into the filling shaft set over a rotating cutting disc. The disc reduces fibres to pulp, from which juice is extracted by centrifugal force through a fine mesh. The pulp remains behind while the juice drips into an integral container that also serves as a pouring jug. The only drawback is that the mesh needs a good scrub to clear it of pulp.

6 Multipurpose kitchen machine This revolutionary machine has a compact motorized base with a universal coupling device to which various attachments are easily fitted. The machine therefore combines several machines in one – the only drawback is its price. The basic model is supplied with a mixing bowl only, which has as accessories a lid, dough hook, double beater and bowl scraper. The more expensive model comes with a blender and food processor, as well as the mixing bowl. Optional extras for both models include a mincer, a continuous shredder and a grain mill.

7 Hand-held mixer Lightweight and compact, the hand-held machine is good for mixing relatively small amounts. The two overlapping steel beaters whisk egg whites into snowy clouds, whip cream and emulsify sauces. You can also use the mixer for creaming butter and sugar, though the beaters get clogged up. Unlike the standing mixer, the hand-held version allows you to control the position of the beaters. You can move them over the edge and base of the mixing bowl so everything is evenly mixed. A switch enables you to alter the speed while mixing.

macadamia nut-crusted chicken breasts
with lemon grass-coconut emulsion

Contributed by award-winning American chef and restaurant owner Charlie Trotter, this dish is rich and delicious, with sensual flavours that harmonize perfectly. The slightly wilted watercress is essential for cutting the richness of the macadamia nuts and balancing all the flavours. Use a hand-held electric blender or mixer to froth up the sauce.

Serves 4

Tools	Ingredients
preparation bowls	400g can coconut milk
cook's knife	225ml milk
vegetable knife	8 stalks chopped lemon grass
small saucepan	1 tbsp rice vinegar
sieve	1 tbsp lemon juice
citrus juicer	1 yellow pepper, halved and deseeded
small bowls for prepared ingredients	50g leek, cut into matchstick strips
small roasting pan	3 1/2 tbsp groundnut or sunflower oil
small frying pan	6cm piece fresh ginger root, peeled and cut into matchstick strips
large frying pan	
perforated turner	4 skinless, boneless chicken breasts, about 150g each
hand-held electric blender or mixer	salt and freshly ground black pepper
	4 tbsp chopped macadamia nuts
	50g trimmed watercress
	2 tbsp shredded coconut, lightly toasted
	2 tbsp chopped chives

1 Simmer the coconut milk, milk and lemon grass in a small saucepan for 15 minutes. Strain through a sieve and pour back into the pan. Add the vinegar and lemon juice, and set the pan aside.

2 Meanwhile, grill the pepper until blackened. Peel off the skin, cut the flesh into matchstick strips and keep warm.

3 Plunge the strips of leek into a pan of boiling water. Bring it back to the boil and boil for a few seconds, then drain the strips and keep warm.

4 Heat 1 1/2 tbsp of the oil in a small frying pan. Add the ginger and fry for a minute or so until just golden. Remove from the pan and keep warm.

5 Season the chicken breasts with salt and pepper, and coat the tops with the nuts. Heat the remaining oil in a large, hot frying pan, add the chicken and cook for 3 minutes on each side or until cooked through. Transfer to a plate and keep warm.

6 Add the watercress to the pan in which you cooked the chicken. Cook it gently for 1 minute or until wilted. Season to taste with salt and pepper.

7 Gently reheat the coconut emulsion, whisking with a hand-held blender or mixer until frothy.

8 To assemble the dish, place some yellow pepper and leek in the middle of each serving bowl. Arrange some of the watercress over the vegetables and top with a chicken breast. Pour the emulsion around each bowl and sprinkle with the fried ginger and toasted coconut. Sprinkle the chives around the emulsion.

grinding grating and crushing

mills, mortars and mincers

These tools change the size and texture of ingredients, usually by abrading or crushing them between two hard surfaces in a closely confined space. A manual or mechanized rotary movement causes friction, which in turn produces the desired grounds, powder or paste.

Using tools of this sort will immeasurably improve the flavour of your cooking, as they allow you to use raw materials rather than processed travesties. Think of the difference between freshly ground black pepper and the brown dust which passes for ready-ground pepper; or between the heady aroma of freshly ground spices and commercial curry powder.

Once crushed or ground, hard-coated ingredients such as coffee beans, peppercorns and other spices release the volatile oils responsible for their distinctive flavours. When they are exposed to the atmosphere, the oils quickly oxidize and lose their pungency. Similarly, the fat in ground or grated Parmesan cheese will oxidize and become rancid before long, and a piece of meat will deteriorate rapidly once ground, because the much greater surface area increases its exposure to the atmosphere and to harmful organisms.

Tools for grinding and grating are therefore invaluable, enabling you to process ingredients at exactly the right moment for maximum flavour and minimum deterioration. Some tools not only grind but also act as storage containers, protecting the contents from the effects of light and air.

Spice mills
1 Liven up your curries with this fifties-style, black-and-chrome spice mill. Its rock-hard ceramic grinding mechanism is designed to cope with dried herbs and spices, as well as salt and pepper. The mechanism is fully adjustable for fine and coarse grinds. To maintain its jazzy good looks, however, the mill needs to be kept scrupulously clean.
2 Less glamorous but equally durable is the Crushgrind® spice mill. It, too, has a ceramic grinding mechanism, but there is no adjustment facility. Even so, the mill does its job remarkably well, and looks no less presentable even after a stint in the kitchen. It is sold either as an empty container or filled with interesting spice blends.

3 Meat grinder A true kitchen classic, this cast-iron, hand-cranked grinder funnels meat into the spiral shaft of a revolving screw. From there, it is forced through rotating blades and finally through a perforated cutting disc. Alternative cutting discs can be fitted to regulate the fineness or coarseness of the end product.

Pepper and salt mills
4 These stylish, polished metal mills have a pull-down 'laundry chute' refilling system that saves unscrewing and dismantling the top. The grinding mechanism, made from high-quality hardened steel, adjusts to produce a range of fine and coarse grounds.
5 Designed in a classic hourglass shape, these wooden mills have a chromed steel band for adjusting the grounds from fine to coarse. The stainless-steel grinding mechanism is constructed in such a way that there is no metal-to-metal contact, and it is therefore unlikely to wear out.

Choosing grinding tools

A pepper mill is a must. Choose one that holds at least three tablespoons of peppercorns, or you will be constantly refilling it. The best mills allow you to control the size of the grounds. Invariably sold as a pair with a pepper mill, a salt mill is useful if you live in a humid climate where caking is likely to be a problem.

No kitchen should be without a pestle and mortar. They perform a variety of tasks – grinding spices, making pesto, crushing garlic, for example – and so reduce the need for several different tools. If you like coffee, a coffee mill will give you the unbeatable aroma and flavour of the drink made with freshly ground beans.

The other mills are a matter of personal choice. Whether you need them depends on how often you use an ingredient, and whether you prefer a mill or a grater. If you regularly use ground meat, for example to make burgers or terrines, it's worth buying a meat grinder. Yes, you have to clamp it to a table and wash the parts after use, but it repays the effort. You can choose a decent cut of meat, there is no risk of contamination from meat that has previously passed through the grinder, and you can add your own seasonings.

6

Mill maintenance

O Use a pepper mill for pepper and a salt mill for salt. If you use salt in a pepper mill it will corrode the metal grinding mechanism. (A salt mill's mechanism is usually made from a non-corroding material such as nylon.)

O Lubricate the top of the spindle, where it meets the adjusting screw, with a drop of cooking oil. This will prevent rusting and keep the thread in good working order.

O Don't mill over open pans as steam causes rusting and dampens the grounds, which can clog up the mechanism. It's better to mill into a large spoon or over a plate or piece of paper, then tip the grounds into the pan.

O Keep mill bodies clean by wiping with a damp cloth. Rub wooden mills with vegetable oil occasionally to prevent the wood from drying out.

Coffee mills
6 Working on the same principle as a blender, the two-armed blade of this electric mill pulverizes coffee beans in seconds. Though it is compact and easy to use, the grounds are uneven in size and you have to guess how long to whizz for. It is also noisy. Coffee mills that produce uniform grounds have grinding wheels rather than blades. They will satisfy purists, but are more complex to use and take up more space.
7 A more leisurely way of grinding beans is with a hand-cranked coffee mill. As you turn the handle, the beans are fed into the hopper and through the metal grinding mechanism. The coffee grounds drop into the receiving drawer below. Based on a traditional design, this clear perspex mill allows you to see the beans being ground. It produces reasonable results, but the grounds are quite coarse.

Pestles and mortars
10 This solid metal pestle and mortar is designed primarily for grinding seeds and spices. The interior of the mortar has a flat base and straight, outwardly sloping sides, instead of the usual rounded bowl shape. The flat-tipped pestle mirrors the shape of the mortar and so maximizes the surface area available for grinding.
11 The ceramic mortar has a slightly abrasive, unglazed surface that grinds both dry and moist ingredients. Smooth mortars made from marble or glazed ceramic should have a ground surface on the inside, otherwise dry foods will slide over the surface.
12 The Japanese mortar (suribachi) has a characteristically wide, shallow bowl, with an interior covered with unglazed ridges running in different directions. Used with the broad-tipped wooden pestle (surikogi), it efficiently grinds oily seeds and raw chopped fish or poultry to a coarse paste.

10   11

12

7   8   9

Nutmeg and Parmesan mills
These mills enable you to use up the last fragment of nutmeg or cheese without grating your fingertips.
8 The stainless-steel Parmesan mill will also grind nutmeg and cheese.
9 The chrome and acrylic nutmeg mill stores up to four additional nutmegs.

Pesto alla Genovese Bruising and pounding fresh basil leaves with a pestle beats any other method. Put 2 good handfuls of torn basil leaves, 2 mashed garlic cloves, 3 tablespoons of pine nuts and a generous pinch of sea salt in a mortar and grind to a paste, moving the pestle around the mortar and crushing the ingredients against the sides. Add 8 tablespoons of freshly grated Parmesan cheese and 2 tablespoons of freshly grated pecorino Romano cheese, grinding until evenly mixed. Beat in 8 tablespoons of extra-virgin olive oil. This makes about 100ml of pesto.

Garam masala Freshly ground garam masala (meaning 'heating spices') lifts a curry from the mundane to the magnificent. A basic mixture includes an equal weight of cinnamon sticks, cloves and black peppercorns, and a small amount of black cardamom seeds. Experiment with additional spices such as dried chillies, and fennel, cumin and coriander seeds. For the best flavour, lightly toast whole spices and grind them to a powder just before use.

Pumpkin purée Cut peeled pumpkin or winter squash into chunks and simmer or steam until tender. Drain well and push through a food mill. The purée can be used to make pumpkin pie. Alternatively, for a colourful soup, dilute to desired thickness with good chicken stock. Add cooked black beans and some roasted mashed chilli. Simmer gently to reheat. Pour into soup bowls and top with crumbled white cheese, pumpkin seeds and a slick of pumpkin-seed oil or extra-virgin sunflower oil.

Fresh tomato juice Slice ripe, flavourful tomatoes in half, and push through a tomato press. For a thicker solution, allow the juice to settle before decanting, then pour off the clear liquid that appears on the surface. If you like, run the seeds and skins through the press again to extract more juice. Add the pulp to the first batch of juice.

coconut vegetable stew

Specializing in the light, home-style cooking of Kerala in south-western India, Das Sreedharan's London-based Rasa chain of restaurants have revealed a very different side to Indian food. This colourful mixture of vegetables, cooked in a subtle blend of freshly ground spices, grated fresh coconut and tangy yogurt, is typical of Keralan cooking. Known as 'avial', it is a traditional festival dish, and no wedding or feast would be complete without it.

Drumsticks, or Indian asparagus, are podded seeds from a tropical tree. The pulp and seeds are sucked out of the cooked pods, rather like eating asparagus. To prepare drumsticks, string them like celery and cut into 2.5–5cm lengths. They have an assertive flavour and some cooks like to parboil them for 10 minutes before proceeding with the recipe.

Green mango has a sour, fruity taste. Both green mango and drumsticks are available from good Asian food stores. If you have difficulty finding them, increase the quantity of the other vegetables, or substitute different ones. Instead of green mango, use a firm ordinary mango tossed with a pinch of citric acid or amchoor powder, available from good supermarkets.

Serves 4 as a side dish

Tools	Ingredients
pestle and mortar	1 tsp cumin seeds
paring knife	2.5cm piece fresh ginger root, roughly chopped
vegetable peeler	
large saucepan	1 green chilli, deseeded and roughly chopped
wooden spoon	
grater	3 small carrots
colander	2 potatoes
	1 small green mango
	100g drumsticks, strings removed
	100g green beans
	20 curry leaves (optional)
	1 tsp ground turmeric
	1 tsp salt, or to taste
	8–10 tbsp thick plain yogurt
	3 tbsp coarsely grated fresh coconut
	few shreds fresh coconut, to garnish

1 Using a pestle and mortar, grind the cumin seeds, ginger root and chilli to a paste with 1 tablespoon of water.
2 Slice the carrots, potatoes and green mango into fingers, 1cm thick and about 5cm long. Slice the drumsticks and beans into 5cm pieces.
3 Put the carrots and drumsticks in a large, heavy-based saucepan with barely enough water to cover – about 300ml. Bring to the boil and simmer, uncovered, for 5 minutes, stirring occasionally to prevent sticking.
4 Add the potatoes and simmer over a medium heat, stirring now and then until nearly cooked, about 5 minutes.
5 Add the green beans, mango and curry leaves, if using, and stir in the turmeric, salt and spice paste. Reduce the heat and simmer for about 5 more minutes with the lid on, stirring occasionally until the vegetables are cooked.
6 Remove the vegetables from the heat and stir in the yogurt and coconut. Reheat gently if necessary but do not allow to simmer or the yogurt will curdle. Garnish with a few coconut shreds before serving.

graters

A grater is essentially a surface covered with rows of small, sharp cutting edges, and as such, it accomplishes the work of a knife in far less time and often with more uniformity. Some graters work in two directions, others in one only. When choosing a metal grater, make sure it is made of stainless steel, otherwise it will rust. To clean stubborn debris from the cutting edges, rinse the grater under running water, then scrub with a nailbrush.

1 Porcelain grater This thick, flat porcelain grater (oroshigane) from Japan is a pleasure to use. Instead of perforations, it has rows of pyramid-like teeth angled in two directions. Used for ginger root and daikon radish, the resulting pulp is moist, flavourful and not at all fibrous. The grater can also be used for nutmeg.

2 Citrus grater Made of acid-resistant stainless steel, the lemon grater has very fine perforations. This enables you to grate the zest, or outer surface of the rind, without taking up any of the bitter pith.

3 Flat graters Flat graters are easy to store. It is better to buy two or three with different cutting surfaces, rather than a single flat grater with several grades, as the area of each will be small. The fine holes of the top grater are ideal for grating hard and semi-hard cheeses. The middle grater has very small toothed rectangular perforations that work in both directions. They reduce dense-fleshed fruit and vegetables such as apples and carrots to a sweet, moist pulp – perfect baby food or muesli topping. The third grater has coarser holes for grating root vegetables.

7 Rotary grater Ideal for thrifty cooks and for children, the rotary grater deals with scraps of cheese and can also be used for carrots, nuts and chocolate. There is no risk of grating your fingertips as the food is pressed against the rotating drum by a wide covering plate at the end of the upper handle. Extra cylinders provide a choice of perforation sizes.

4 Box grater A box grater provides the greatest choice of cutting surfaces, ranging from very fine to coarse. It also has a slot for slicing cucumbers or shaving Parmesan. The rectangular base makes the grater self-supporting, which allows you to exert downward pressure more easily. The disadvantage is that the boxy shape makes it awkward to remove the raspings from the inside. This grater is also bulky to store and may not fit easily into a drawer.

5 Microplane® grater This state-of-the-art grater has rows of minute, ultra-sharp blades that cut food precisely and cleanly with no shredding, tearing or clogging. No pressure is required from the user. It has two drawbacks: the price, and the fact that you have to buy two graters if you want a choice of fine and coarse perforations.

6 Nutmeg grater Freshly grated nutmeg has a much better taste and aroma than the pre-ground sort, so it is worth investing in a special grater or mill. The nutmeg grater has very fine perforations and a curved surface, both of which reduce the risk of grated fingertips.

Grating vegetables

Coarsely grating vegetables such as courgettes is an excellent way of ensuring they cook evenly and fast, whether boiled, steamed, braised or stir-fried. To stir-fry, tip the grated vegetables into a pan in which you have melted a knob of butter with a little olive oil. Stir-fry for 2–3 minutes, seasoning to taste.

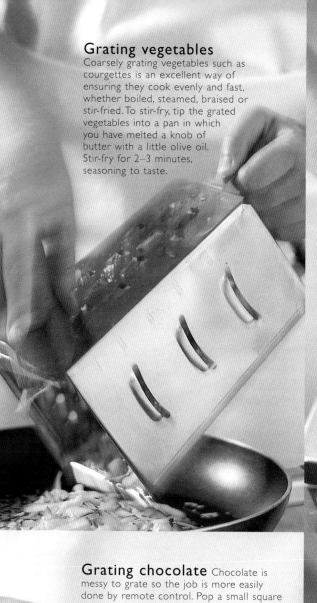

Grating nutmeg
Nutmeg is at its most aromatic when freshly grated. Use a small fine-holed grater and grate directly over the food. Here a creamy rice pudding is prepared for the oven prior to baking. Cooked spinach, pasta tossed in cream, hot toddies, and cappuccino are also enhanced with freshly grated nutmeg.

Grating chocolate
Chocolate is messy to grate so the job is more easily done by remote control. Pop a small square into a rotary grater and grate directly over desserts such as ice-cream sundaes. A little goes a long way and the tool is particularly useful for those who enjoy chocolate but need to watch their weight.

Grating fruit
Dense-fleshed fruits such as apples and pears are easier for some people to digest if they are very finely grated. A grater with sharp, fine blades, such as the Microplane®, makes light work of the firmest apple, and is ideal for grating fruit over muesli, or making fruit purées for older babies and toddlers.

mashers, crushers and crackers

These invaluable tools break down the texture of raw or cooked food so that it becomes more palatable. They tenderize tough fibres such as those in raw meat, pierce thick skins, smash impenetrable nuts or lobsters and produce delectable mashes and purées. These tools are not mere gadgets. They have stood the test of time and they do their job efficiently and well. Although their basic structure and function have not altered through the ages, many of these items are produced in stylish modern designs that complement today's kitchens.

1 Tomato press
A good old-fashioned machine that conveniently separates juice and pulp from seeds and peel. As you turn the handle, the flanged drum catches and traps halved tomatoes, pressing them onto a perforated plate that funnels the liquid down a chute. A second flange sweeps the solids towards another chute. It is not very easy to clean, but well worth having if your garden produces a fair-sized tomato harvest.

3 Garlic press This sleek, space-age garlic press works in exactly the same way as a traditional one. A flat-faced pusher forces peeled or unpeeled garlic through the holes in the bowl of the press. Some presses have an extra protuberance and bowl for pitting olives or cherries, for example. Others have a spiked self-cleaning device that pushes out every bit of debris from the holes.

4 Vegetable press The wide, gently curved, perforated surface is rocked over soft-textured vegetables and fruit, reducing them to a rough pulp. The wooden handles on this one make the press comfortable to hold and help to exert downward pressure, but the receiving bowl needs to be wide and shallow so the handles do not hit the sides. Some models have a U-shaped handle, which is less comfortable to hold but perhaps more convenient.

2 Meat mallet/tenderizer
This hefty lump of cast aluminium is used for pounding and tenderizing meat. The notches on one side break down the fibres; the smooth side bashes the meat flat.

5 Food mill Used for mincing fruit and vegetables, this mill has different-textured metal sieving discs that fit in the base. A metal blade on top of the disc forces the food through as you turn the handle. The texture of the food depends on whether you use a disc with fine, medium or coarse perforations. There is even a small model for puréeing baby foods.

6 Potato ricer The potato ricer makes lumpy mash a thing of the past. Peeled, boiled potato is squeezed through a mesh of tiny holes to emerge looking like grains of soft rice. The ricer can be used for mashing all kinds of root vegetables and cooked apples too.

7 Potato masher The potato masher breaks down lumps as you pound. Its main advantage is that potatoes can be mashed in the pan in which they were cooked. Like the potato ricer, it can be used to mash any kind of starchy root vegetable or dense-fleshed cooked fruit.

Nutcrackers

8 The hinged cone nutcracker is designed to accommodate a variety of nuts, both large and small. Furrowed gripping surfaces hold the nuts firmly in place while you crack them open.

9 The ratchet cracker does all the work for you. Simply place the nut between the ratchet and the top of the crackers and work the ratchet up with the lever until the shell cracks and falls apart.

10 The hinged pincer type requires some pressure to use but the pleasure of extracting a whole kernel is worth the effort.

11 Lobster/crab crackers
Resembling lobster claws, these crackers work in the same way as hinged nutcrackers. The inside edges are ridged so you can grip unyielding lobster or crab claws firmly enough to crack them.

Citrus presses

12 This sturdy little, cone-shaped press is ideal for limes or small lemons. It squeezes out every drop of juice minus the pips, and also squeezes out oils, giving the juice a more intense flavour. The press has a special silicone coating to prevent corrosion and discolouration from fruit acid.

13 A chrome body and an easy-to-grip matt black handle are an update on the time-honoured wooden reamer. The tapered tip penetrates the flesh while the furrows crush and squeeze out the juice as the cone is turned. The reamer literally screws the juice out of half lemons or limes.

14 This glass lemon squeezer is of a traditional design. Place halved fruit over the dome and then press and twist to extract the juice. The pointed teeth arranged around the base of the dome prevent pips from trespassing into the juice-collecting gutter.

15 This magnificent, tall, chrome citrus press is for serious juicing. Place half an orange or large lemon in the press, pull down the handle and the geared mechanism will extract every drop of juice from the fruit.

basic mashed potato

Though it seems simple, producing a mound of light, airy, lump-free mashed potato requires a little know-how. Variety of potato is important – use a floury type with a distinctive flavour (see Ingredients). Some cooks argue that it is better to boil potatoes unpeeled so water cannot penetrate and cause a waterlogged mash. I have tried boiling the same variety of potato with and without its skin, and cannot honestly detect any noticeable difference. When you are ready to mash, use a potato masher, or, for a creamier result, a potato ricer or food mill. Never use a food processor – unless you want wallpaper paste.

a   b

Tools	Ingredients
saucepan with a lid	1kg evenly sized floury potatoes such as Kerr's Pink, Wilja or King Edward, peeled or unpeeled
colander	
clean tea towel	salt
potato masher, ricer or food mill	100g butter, softened at room temperature and cut into pieces
wooden spoon or balloon whisk	150–300ml hot milk

1 Put the potatoes in a saucepan with enough water to just cover them. Add 1 tablespoon of salt and cover with a tight-fitting lid. Bring to the boil, then simmer gently, with the lid in place, until tender – about 20 minutes. Drain well, peel if necessary and put back in the pan. Cover with a clean tea towel for a minute or two to get rid of excess moisture.

2 For coarse-textured mash, bash the potatoes and butter with a masher (a). Season to taste with sea salt and freshly ground black pepper.

3 For a smoother, fluffier mash, add some hot milk and, using a wooden spoon or balloon whisk, beat until you can beat no more (b). Add extra milk if needed.

sweet potato mash with chilli and sizzled ginger

This flavoursome variation on mashed potato is delicious served with spicy grilled chicken, lamb or fish. You can of course use ordinary potatoes, but sweet potato goes particularly well with ingredients such as ginger and chilli, which share its tropical origins.

Serves 4 as a side dish

Tools	Ingredients
vegetable peeler	1.25kg orange-fleshed sweet potatoes, peeled and cut into even-sized pieces
cook's knife	
saucepan with a lid	
colander	sea salt flakes and freshly ground black pepper
clean tea towel	4 tbsp chopped fresh coriander
potato masher	2 tbsp butter
wooden spoon	40g piece fresh ginger root, sliced into matchsticks, 2.5cm long
medium frying pan	
	1/2 red chilli, deseeded and very finely chopped

1 Cook the sweet potatoes following step 1 of 'basic mashed potato' above. They may need a little less cooking time than ordinary potatoes.

2 Bash the potatoes with a masher to break up the lumps. Season with sea salt and freshly ground black pepper and stir in the coriander. Spoon into a warmed serving dish.

3 Heat the butter in a frying pan. When it is sizzling, throw in the ginger and chilli. Fry for a minute or two until the ginger is golden. Pour over the potato, stir to partially mix, and serve at once.

mixing and whisking

bowls

Bowls are the nuts and bolts of kitchen utensils. After all, if you didn't have some sort of receptacle to mix, store or serve in, how would meals ever be prepared? Bowls come in a wide range of materials: glass, copper, stainless steel, aluminium, enamel, ceramic, earthenware, melamine and polyethylene. As with knives, you will need a variety of shapes and sizes for different tasks.

Bowls are vital for orderly, well-organized meal preparation. Get in the habit of preparing all your ingredients before you start to cook, and have them ready and waiting in appropriate bowls. Your 'prep' bowls should include several small ones for ingredients like chopped garlic and ginger. Equally vital are three or four 1- to 4-litre bowls that can double up as serving bowls. If you regularly whisk egg whites or batters, you'll need a bowl that is deep enough to stop the mixture splattering your kitchen. You may want to treat yourself to a copper bowl for egg whites – your meringues will be unrivalled. Not absolutely essential, but useful nevertheless, is a big ceramic bowl for the occasional large mixing task such as making a Christmas cake.

1

3

5

1 Basic glass bowl This plain glass bowl has a rolled rim for easy pouring. It comes with a plastic lid and is available in several sizes.

2 Duralex 9-piece set A bowl for every occasion, made from heat-tempered, oven- and microwave-proof glass. Use them for preparation, cooking, serving and storing. This is a useful set to have if your storage space is limited.

3 Stainless-steel bowls Stainless-steel is the ideal material for food preparation bowls as it is resistant to acid and is not tainted by smells. Pristine, shiny and indestructible, these bowls are so elegant you won't want to put them away. Use them for preparation, serving and storage.

4 Copper bowl An essential piece of equipment for meringue makers, this bowl transforms egg whites into billowing clouds of stable foam like no other bowl, thanks to the alchemy that takes place between copper and egg whites (see 'miraculous meringue', page 49). The sloping sides and rounded base make for effortless whisking, while the bowl's generous diameter allows for rapid expansion of foam. The most useful size is about 30cm in diameter. Make sure your bowl has a rolled rim to keep its shape, and a hook so you can show it off on the wall.

5 Melamine bowl Rigid, tough and practically unbreakable, melamine makes ideal bowl material. This one is gleamingly smooth, with a handy pouring lip and a rubber-rimmed base that prevents slipping. It is available in three sizes and a range of cheerful colours.

6 Ceramic bowl This traditional mixing bowl is made of glazed ceramic. The flattened area on the side keeps the bowl steady when it is tilted at an angle as you beat.

2

4

6

spoons

Together with bowls and knives, spoons are among the earliest and most basic kitchen tools. They are essential for any job involving mixing, and in many ways are simply a replacement for the hand. They stir, beat, scoop and scrape, and can also be used as a measuring tool.

Wooden spoons are a must. They are strong, inflexible and poor conductors of heat. You can leave a wooden spoon in a pan of simmering soup without fear of the handle heating up; nor will it bend or snap while you stir dense mixtures such as fruit cake. The curved back of a wooden spoon is perfect for pressing moisture out of cooked spinach, and for pushing soft fruit through a sieve. The handle can be used for moulding shaped biscuits such as brandy snaps or cannoli.

Though they may look somewhat crude, wooden spoons are subtly designed to perform a range of different tasks, so it is worth collecting a variety of sizes and shapes. Keep your spoons within easy reach of the stove. Those made from hardwoods, such as beech or boxwood, are strong and taint-free. Pine or other softwoods can impart a resinous smell to food, and they also have a tendency to splinter and crack. Always wash and dry wooden spoons thoroughly after you use them, and preferably allow them to air.

A long-handled, large metal spoon is another must. The thin edge delicately cuts through airy mixtures such as whisked egg whites so they don't collapse as you fold in other ingredients. Use a metal spoon also for basting meat – the long handle will protect you from the heat – and for serving rice – the thin edge will not break up delicate grains as you scoop them up. Buy a spoon that you can hang on a hook, ready for its thousand and one uses.

Wooden spoons

1 A spoon with a straight edge and angled point fits snugly into the corners of a flat-bottomed pan, while the curved side copes with rounded pans. The blunt end can be used to shunt food around a sauté pan and dislodge sticky sediment from the base. This is a good spoon for making gravy.

2 This traditional wooden spoon is an essential tool. It is made of beech and has a beautifully curved oval bowl with thick sides.

3 This smaller basic wooden spoon is made of closely grained golden boxwood. The bowl is a similar shape to the beech spoon (2).

4 A long-handled spoon (at least 40cm) is ideal for stirring continuously over furnace-like heat – when using a wok, for instance – or for stirring polenta.

5 Metal mixing spoon With its perfect oval bowl and long handle, this metal spoon is of a high quality. Made from a single piece of metal, the handle will not work loose from the bowl.

6 Wire mixing spoon This stylish spoon is used with rounded pans. The outer wire skims over any crust that may have built up on the pan base without incorporating it into the mixture. The thicker inner wire is strong enough for mixing, lifting and turning. The spoon can also be used for whisking.

7 Scoop Useful for shovelling up dry goods such as flour or grains, the scoop has a straight-sided, deep bowl that holds a generous amount without spilling. Traditionally made of tinned steel, scoops such as this will rust if used for moist foods.

8 Insulated ice-cream scoop Made of seamless aluminium and filled with salt-based defrosting fluid, this tool is ideal for late-night ice-cream snacks. The tapered rim easily penetrates hard-packed ice-cream. It is not dishwasher proof.

ladles and spatulas

Ladles are needed for transferring measured amounts of liquid or semi-liquid food. They are invariably brought to the table, so buy a presentable one. To be avoided at all costs are ladles with painted wooden handles – they are guaranteed to flake or work loose. Make sure the bowl has a lip or continuous rolled edge for spill-free pouring. Hanging hooks are also useful.

Spatulas have virtually the same uses as spoons – they stir, mix, fold and scrape, push things through sieves and lift food from pans. Some cooks prefer a wooden spatula to a wooden spoon. One of the advantages of a spatula is that, being flat, it does not harbour clumps of unmixed food. You can also scrape it clean against the edge of the pan. Spatulas come in different materials and shapes. As with spoons, it's useful to have a selection for different tasks.

Ladles

1 Salad dressing ladle This ladle has a vertical handle that allows you to dip it into a tall, narrow container. The angle of the handle also makes it easier to pour with care over food that has been arranged on a plate. The bowl has a two-sided lip, designed for right- and left-handed use.

2 Portioning ladle The 6cm bowl has a pouring lip on each side that enables you to pour with precision, and is designed for right- and left-handed use.

3 Soup ladle A generous 9cm bowl will hold nearly 150ml of liquid – ideal for serving soup. The bowl has a continuous rolled lip to prevent drips, and the handle has a hanging hook that stops the ladle from becoming submerged should you leave it sitting in a large pot of liquid.

4 Chinese wok ladle The wide, shallow bowl is perfect for lifting, tossing and turning the contents of a wok. The long handle distances you from the heat, and the 50° angle mirrors the contours of the wok, making the ladle more comfortable to use. Choose a stainless-steel ladle rather than rust-prone carbon steel.

Spatulas

5 Rubber spatula Shaped more like a spoon, this flexible spatula combines the benefits of a slightly concave bowl with straight edges and rounded corners. It will scrape clean a mixing bowl or pan without scratching.

6 Plastic spatula Available in three sizes, the flexible, fine-edged blade cleanly removes the very last scrap of mixture from a bowl, jar or food processor goblet. One side deals with angled corners, the other with rounded.

7 Coloured plastic spatula Similar in design and function, the coloured spatula has the added benefit of being heat resistant. It will not melt or discolour, even at very high temperatures, nor will it damage non-stick cookware. It is available in a range of colours and sizes.

8 Wooden spatula The slightly angled end is useful for scraping mixtures out of corners and shunting food around the pan. More importantly, the blunt edges will not scratch a non-stick surface, however firmly you scrape.

risotto with red wine and sausages

Australian food writer Jill Dupleix cannot cook without a wooden spoon: 'It beats, it mashes, it stirs, it crushes garlic. It's a tasting spoon, a scraper, a risotto spoon, a porridge spoon, a salad server....Wooden spoons are like tea towels – no matter how many you have in the house, you will use them all.' She puts her spoon to good use in this recipe. Keep the stock simmering in a small saucepan so it is hot when you add it to the rice.

Serves 4

Tools	Ingredients
medium non-stick frying pan	275g Italian pork sausages, or coarse-grained pure pork sausages
cook's knife	I tbsp extra-virgin olive oil
large heavy-based sauté pan	2 tbsp butter
wooden spoon	I onion, finely chopped
small saucepan	300g arborio rice
ladle	200ml red wine
grater	1.3 litres light chicken stock, preferably home-made, heated
	2 tbsp freshly grated Parmesan cheese
	sea salt
	freshly ground black pepper
	Parmesan shavings and small rosemary sprig, to garnish

1 Take the skin off the sausages and pinch the meat into a heated non-stick frying pan. Fry the meat until crusty and golden, then drain off the oil and set the meat aside.

2 Heat the olive oil and half the butter in a heavy-based sauté pan. Fry the onion gently until softened but not browned. Add the rice and, using a wooden spoon, toss well until the rice is coated in the buttery onions. Pour in the red wine and bring to the boil, stirring.

3 Using a ladle, add 125ml of hot chicken stock to the rice. Stir carefully and calmly with a wooden spoon over a medium heat. When the stock has been absorbed by the rice, add another 125ml. From now on it is all in the timing. Add stock, a ladleful at a time, only when the previous stock has been absorbed by the rice. Keep the rice moving in the pan. If you go through a lot of stock quickly, the heat may be too high. If the rice doesn't absorb the stock easily, the heat may be too low.

4 After 20 minutes, add the sausage meat and stir for another 10 minutes until the rice is cooked but not soft, and there is a general creaminess to the sauce; it should be neither soupy nor dry.

5 Turn off the heat. Add the Parmesan, the remaining butter, and sea salt and freshly ground pepper to taste, and stir it through. Cover and leave to rest for 3–4 minutes before serving. Garnish with a rosemary sprig and a few Parmesan shavings. Serve with plenty of red wine on the side (to drink, naturally).

whisks

Air is the least recognized – but one of the most fundamental – ingredients in cooking, and, as we need a means of incorporating it into food, the whisk could rightly be called the most fundamental of tools.

A whisk works by cutting at high speed through egg whites, batters, sauces and other ingredients, not only incorporating air but also performing other vital functions. A whisk smoothes out lumps and uneven concentrations. It breaks down fat globules so they emulsify with non-fat liquids – oil and vinegar in a salad dressing, for example. A whisk also 'denatures' proteins – think of egg whites and the way a viscous mess miraculously turns into a frothy cloud. In this case, the whisk cuts through interwoven strands of protein molecules in unbeaten egg white, effectively chopping them into tiny pieces and introducing air at the same time.

There are a number of shapes and sizes of whisk, designed for a variety of jobs. If choice is restricted, however, a balloon whisk and possibly a small flat whisk are the ones to go for. Choose ones made of stainless steel rather than tin plate, which is likely to discolour and rust. The handle should be comfortably thick and sit well in the hand, and, in the interests of hygiene, should be well sealed at both ends. The wires should be firmly welded in place.

1   2   3   4   5   6

3 Twirl whisk
Also called a whip, this is made from one piece of coiled wire, which gives it greater flexibility. Though the shape makes it useful for working into corners and round the entire base of a container, it is not as efficient as a balloon or egg whisk. It is good for whisking in slim containers, however.

4 Spiral whisk
A spiral whisk is made from a coil of fine, springy wire, looped round a circular wire frame. It can be used in a small amount of liquid, so is invaluable for whisking sauces in shallow pans. This whisk also incorporates mixture from around the edge of the mixing bowl.

5 Jug whisk
Not essential but nevertheless useful, the long jug whisk comes in handy for whisking in narrow glasses, measuring jugs and cocktail shakers.

6 Flat whisk
This whisk is excellent for mixing small amounts, or for beating a single egg yolk, stirring delicate items or mixing herbs into cream.

1 Balloon whisk
The balloon whisk's slightly flexible wires will effectively aerate anything from egg whites to heavy cream. Their bulbous shape increases the area that is in contact with the mixture, so the more wires the better.

2 Egg whisk The egg or sauce whisk is designed to mix, emulsify and aerate egg-based sauces. More elongated and rigid than a balloon whisk, the wires cut through egg proteins in a hollandaise sauce, for example, preventing coagulation and curdling.

spicy prawn pancakes with coriander sauce

For successful pancakes, use a balloon whisk, which effectively mixes and aerates the batter, and smooths out lumps. Do not over-beat or your pancakes will be tough. Use a small, heavy pan that conducts heat evenly and does not stick. A crêpe pan or a well-seasoned omelette pan is ideal.

Makes 8 pancakes

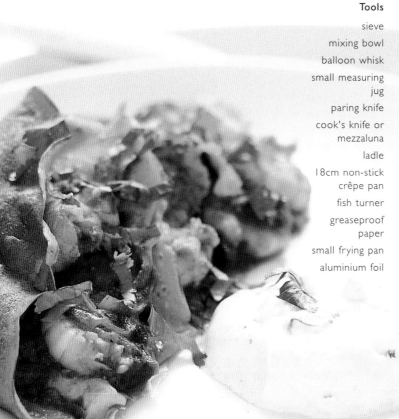

Tools	Ingredients
sieve	100g unbleached plain flour
mixing bowl	pinch of salt
balloon whisk	1 egg, plus 1 egg yolk
small measuring	300ml milk
jug	1 tbsp vegetable oil or melted butter
paring knife	1 1/2 tsp ground turmeric
cook's knife or	vegetable oil, for frying
mezzaluna	*For the sauce:*
ladle	1 garlic clove, finely chopped
18cm non-stick	3 tbsp chopped fresh coriander
crêpe pan	200ml wholemilk yogurt
fish turner	1/2 tsp freshly ground cumin
greaseproof	sea salt and freshly ground black pepper
paper	*For the filling:*
small frying pan	1 tbsp vegetable oil
aluminium foil	1/2 onion, finely chopped
	2 tsp red Thai curry paste
	225g canned chopped tomatoes with juice
	sea salt
	24 large peeled tiger prawns
	1 tbsp lemon juice
	2 tbsp chopped fresh coriander

1 Sift the flour and salt into a bowl. Make a well in the centre and add the egg and extra yolk (a). Add half the milk and whisk well (b). Continue to whisk, gradually adding the rest of the milk, until the batter is smooth. Pour into a small measuring jug and set aside.

2 Mix together all the ingredients for the sauce. Leave to stand to allow the flavours to develop.

3 Whisk the vegetable oil or melted butter into the batter along with the turmeric. Heat enough oil to lightly film an 18cm frying pan. When the oil is hot but not smoking, quickly add a small ladleful of batter, tilting and turning the pan as you do so (c). Fry quickly over a medium-high heat until set on top and brown underneath. Using a fish turner or a quick flip of the pan, turn the pancake and cook until the underside is brown.

4 Transfer the pancake to a plate and keep warm. Repeat, using the remaining batter, to make seven more pancakes. Stack the pancakes with a sheet of greaseproof paper between each one. Cover with foil and keep warm.

5 To make the filling, heat the oil in a small frying pan and gently fry the onion until golden. Add the curry paste and stir-fry for 1 minute. Stir in the tomatoes and season with salt to taste. Simmer for 1–2 minutes. Add the prawns, lemon juice and coriander. Simmer for a few minutes until the prawns are thoroughly heated through.

6 Fold the pancakes in half, and then in half again to make quadrant-shaped cones. Spoon the filling into the top pocket. Arrange in a warmed serving dish or on individual plates, and top with a spoonful of sauce.

Crisp and chewy on the outside, soft as clouds within, meringues have been known to induce cries of ecstasy even from those who are normally unenthusiastic about desserts.

passion-fruit pavlova

The meringue mixture for a pavlova includes cornflour and vinegar, which produce the characteristic texture – crunchy on the outside and soft within. To balance the sweetness of meringue, I have added passion-fruit juice to the cream and topped the pavlova with a selection of luscious tart fruits. Shreds of caramelized orange peel make the pavlova sparkle and add texture. Allow several hours for making the base as it needs to dry thoroughly. Don't worry if it cracks – that's part of the pavlova's characteristic appearance. Serve the finished dish within an hour of assembling it, otherwise it will become soggy.

Serves 8–10

Tools	Ingredients
silicone paper	6 large egg whites
25cm plate	pinch of salt
baking sheet	300g caster sugar, plus 2 tbsp
small bowl	1 1/2 tsp cornflour, sifted
copper bowl or large mixing bowl	1 1/2 tsp white-wine vinegar
	300ml double cream
balloon whisk or hand-held electric mixer	sieved juice from 6 passion fruit
large metal spoon	peel from 1 small orange without any pith, sliced into thin shreds
fine sieve	4 tbsp grenadine syrup
palette knife	1 small papaya
mixing bowl	1 small star fruit
cook's knife	4 kumquats, thinly sliced
nylon sieve for straining passion-fruit pulp	4 physalis, husks removed and fruits halved
wooden spoon	
small saucepan	
tongs	
swivel peeler	

1 Preheat the oven to 150°C/gas 2. Draw a 25cm circle on a sheet of silicone paper, tracing round a plate. Place the paper on a baking sheet, marked side down, so no ink transfers to the base of the meringue.

2 Make the meringue mixture following steps 1–4 for 'basic meringue' (see opposite), using the 300g of caster sugar. Sprinkle the cornflour and vinegar over the foam and gently fold in.

3 Spoon the meringue onto the traced circle, using a palette knife to level the top and smooth the sides (a).

4 Place the baking sheet in the oven and immediately turn the heat down to 140°C/gas 1. Bake for 1 1/4 hours until the meringue is firm. Turn the oven off but leave the meringue inside with the door closed until the oven is completely cool.

5 An hour before assembling, whip the cream, then fold in the passion-fruit juice and the 2 tablespoons of sugar. Cover and put in the fridge to chill.

6 Blanch the orange-peel shreds in boiling water for 3 minutes. Drain and tip back into the pan. Add 150ml of fresh water and the grenadine syrup. Simmer briskly for 12–15 minutes until syrupy, but still with some liquid left in the pan. Fish out the shreds with tongs and place on a metal plate to cool, separating any clumps.

7 Cut the papaya in half lengthways and scrape out the seeds, leaving a smooth cavity. Carefully remove the peel, then place each half on a board cut-side down and slice crossways into thin crescents. Cut the crescents into two or three neat pieces, depending on the size.

8 Cut the star fruit in half and reserve one half for another use. Using a swivel peeler, shave off the dark stripe along the edge of the ribs. Slice the flesh thinly into about eight slices.

9 Place the meringue base on a serving plate. Spoon the cream over the meringue, spreading it out with a palette knife. Arrange the fruits on top, scatter with the orange-peel shreds, and carry proudly to the table.

miraculous meringue

Air and egg whites beaten together with sugar produce one of life's miracles – a snowy foam, which when slowly baked in the oven is transformed into utterly irresistible, melt-in-the-mouth meringue.

Making meringue is simple if you follow a few basic rules. Bowl and beaters must be scrupulously clean – if there is the slightest trace of grease or moisture the egg whites won't whisk properly. Egg whites even absorb moisture from the atmosphere, so don't make meringues on a humid or rainy day or they'll end up 'weeping' small beads of moisture.

Temperature is important too. Egg whites at room temperature have a lower surface tension than those straight from the fridge. A relaxed gel allows air to be beaten in more easily, which, results in a higher volume of foam. Separate the whites from the yolks an hour or so before whisking. Crack the eggs carefully as the yolk is 30 per cent fat and even a speck will contaminate the whites. Break each white into a separate bowl before adding it to the rest, so any mishaps with yolks affect only one egg.

The mixing bowl is all-important. It must be large enough to allow spirited whisking and the expansion of foam. Ideally, the base should be spherical so foam does not get trapped in a corner. Use a bowl made of glass, ceramic or stainless steel rather than plastic, which is hard to keep completely grease-free. Best of all is an unlined copper bowl. A chemical reaction between the metal and the egg whites strengthens the bubbles, producing a creamier, more stable foam. However, if you leave the whites in a copper bowl more than 15 minutes, another reaction takes place that turns them an unappetizing grey. To avoid this, clean the bowl before you use it with a tablespoon of salt and the juice of half a lemon or a tablespoon of vinegar. Rub the mixture round the bowl with your fingers. Rinse the bowl with hot water and dry with a clean cloth.

basic meringue

The ratio of sugar to egg white is normally 50g caster sugar per white; more sugar can be used if you want a harder meringue.

Makes 600ml

Tools	Ingredients
small bowl	4 egg whites
large mixing bowl	pinch of salt
balloon whisk or hand-held electric mixer	200g caster sugar
large metal spoon	

1 Separate the eggs, pour the whites into a large clean bowl and add a pinch of salt. This helps keep the foam stable. Using the whisk or hand-held mixer, beat gently until the whites begin to change into a frothy foam.

2 Now beat rapidly with a circular motion that lifts the whites and incorporates air, until you have a uniformly foamy mass. When you lift some of the white with the whisk it should form a soft, droopy peak (a). At this stage the foam can be used for soufflés and mousses.

3 For baked meringue, continue to beat until the foam forms stiff, pointy peaks. Do not overbeat at this stage or you will end up with dry lumps of foam. Add half the caster sugar, a spoonful at a time, beating well after each addition. The foam should now be smooth and shiny (b).

4 Using a large metal spoon, lightly and evenly fold in the rest of the sugar (c). Use right away, as the mixture quickly starts to liquefy.

Sabayon sauce Use a large balloon whisk to make a light, sweet sauce to serve with hot pies and puddings, or to spoon over summer berries. Put 3 large free-range egg yolks, 50g of caster sugar and 100ml of sparkling white wine into a large heatproof bowl or zabaglione pan (see page 69). Set this over a saucepan of gently simmering water. Beat the mixture steadily until it increases in volume and becomes a firm but light and creamy foam that forms a trail when the whisk is lifted. **Serves 4**

Mayonnaise Use an egg whisk or sauce whisk to make creamy mayonnaise for salads and dips. Put 2 free-range egg yolks, 1/4 teaspoon of sea salt, 1/4 teaspoon of mustard powder, a little freshly ground black pepper and 1/2 teaspoon of olive or sunflower oil into a medium-size bowl. Beat until smooth, then beat in another 1/2 teaspoon of oil. Continue adding oil in tiny amounts, increasing the flow as the mixture thickens. You will need a total of 250ml of oil. Finally, mix in 1 tablespoon of white-wine vinegar and 1 tablespoon of warm water. Check the seasoning. To make aïoli, add 5–6 garlic cloves, pounded to a paste with sea salt, at the start and omit the vinegar. **Makes about 350ml.**
Note this contains raw eggs, which can be hazardous to young children, pregnant women and the elderly.

sieving and straining

sieves, sifters and dredgers

These tools refine the texture of food. They smooth lumps and coarse particles from free-flowing powders such as flour or icing sugar; and they indirectly lighten mixtures, because the process of sieving or sifting helps to incorporate air as the powder floats down into the receiving bowl.

Sieves are additionally used to separate solids from liquids, as in draining peas, or to alter the texture of food. For example, hard-boiled egg yolk can be transformed into a mimosa-like garnish by pushing it through a fine-meshed sieve. Raspberries can be divested of their seeds in the same way. A sieve is also useful for rescuing lumpy gravy or a béchamel sauce that is not as smooth as it should be – place the sieve over a clean saucepan, pour the mixture into the sieve, and smooth out the lumps by pressing with the back of a wooden spoon.

A sieve should sit comfortably over the receiving container. Conical sieves work best with tall containers; bowl-shaped sieves are best used with bowls. The container needs to be large and deep enough to accommodate both the depth of the sieve and the depth of the ingredients once sieved. Don't sift dry powder in a damp sieve as you'll end up with paste. Nor is it advisable to sieve seedy or fibrous food through an ultra-fine sieve – it will be very difficult to clean. If you do need to clean fibrous material from a sieve, hold it under running water with the inside facing down and scrub the outside of the sieve with a nail brush. Turn the sieve bowl-side up, scrub the inside and rinse again.

1 Dredgers A dredger is used to store and dispense flour (large holes) or sugar (small). Turn the dredger upside down and shake it like a salt cellar. The top unscrews for filling. When refilling a sugar dredger, take care not to let the crystals stick to the thread. They will cause problems with screwing and unscrewing.

2 Drum sieve Used in India and known as a 'tamis' in France, this sieve has a closely woven mesh stretched tightly over its circular frame. Frames come in wood, plastic or metal, and in a wide range of diameters. Meshes are made of nylon, silk or metal, and are usually interchangeable. Depending on the closeness of the weave, the sieve removes lumps from powders and coarse particles from spices and grains. A drum sieve is useful for sieving large amounts, as ingredients pass through a flat mesh more quickly than a concave one. However, dry ingredients tend to randomly sprinkle over a wide area, which may be a problem if you want to confine them to a small space.

3 Flour sifter This spring-set sifter aerates clumpy flour to a light, uniform consistency. It has a fine-meshed base with spokes set above it that agitate the flour as you press the trigger in the handle. The process is somewhat laborious, so the tool is suitable for sifting small quantities of flour only. Try to refrain from washing it, as a damp sifter turns flour to paste. It will remain clean enough if you store it in a plastic bag in a cupboard or drawer.

Choosing sieves Essential are two or three medium-to-large bowl-shaped sieves; then you will always have a dry one ready for use. A large sieve, measuring about 24cm in diameter, is worth having for sieving any reasonable quantity of flour or icing sugar. If the sieve is too small, the powder tends to either spill over the edge of the sieve or float into the atmosphere; a sieve with a generous-sized bowl will keep it in place. A couple of smaller sieves, about 10–12cm in diameter, are useful for directing powder or liquid into a narrow-necked container such as a measuring jug. Essential for sieving soft fruits or removing pips from citrus juice is a fine-meshed sieve made of nylon, which, unlike metal, does not react with the acid in the fruit.

When buying, check the sieve has an ear or lip to rest on the edge of the container. Also, check the strength of the mesh, as this will take the brunt of the pressure when you work foods through it. The weakest point is the base of the bowl, which may eventually wear out.

4

4 Nylon sieve A nylon sieve is non-corroding and therefore preferable for sieving acidic foods that might be tainted by metal. It is moulded from one piece of plastic, and therefore has no joints to break or work loose. This sieve will last a lifetime, so choose a colour you can live with.

5   **6**   **7**

Bowl-shaped sieves
The very fine mesh of these attractive stainless-steel sieves is ideal for sifting flour, icing sugar and other fine powders.
5 The larger sieve can also be used to drain small amounts of vegetables.
6 The small sieve is useful for sprinkling icing sugar over cakes, as it enables you to aim more accurately.

7 Chinois sieve and pestle Also called a 'bouillon strainer', this conical sieve funnels liquids downwards into the tip for more accurate pouring. The ultra-fine, twill-like mesh clears stocks of every sediment, and strains sauces to velvety smoothness. The sieve is sturdily made with a wide top band to which are welded the handle, hook and frame. The frame protects the mesh from damage.

The pestle is tapered to fit into the bottom of the sieve. Use it to extract flavoursome juices from solid matter, and to produce a very thin purée from softened vegetables – great for thickening and flavouring sauces.

strainers and skimmers

Though the terms 'sieve' and 'strain' may be used interchangeably, a strainer usually has a coarser mesh than a sieve, or holes. It is used mainly to separate solids from liquids. Skimmers remove sediment, fat and scum from the surface of liquids.

A colander is essential. If you cook for crowds, make large amounts of stock, or regularly make pasta for four or more people, you will need one at least 28cm in diameter. It should have feet or a solid base so both your hands are free for lifting the pan from which you are pouring the food. Smaller colanders do not need feet, but should have a sturdy lip and a handle for resting on the receiving utensil. The base should be fairly flat so food at the bottom is not crushed. To drain efficiently, a colander needs a generous number of holes that are reasonably-sized but not so large that peas slip through them. Check they are evenly distributed and come up the sides of the colander.

If you enjoy properly dressed salads, a spinner for drying leaves is another must. A collapsible wire basket is attractive, but does not do as good a job as an enclosed spinner that strains by centrifugal force. Some spinners have a perforated base – the idea being that you hold it over the sink, and spin and drain in one go. I usually end up showering my feet because I forget the base is perforated, so I prefer a spinner with a solid base.

Other essential straining tools are a large perforated metal spoon (look for one that is made from a single piece of metal) and, if you make tea with loose leaves, a tea strainer.

1 Cheesecloth A lightweight cloth that filters out fine sediment from stocks or clarified butter. Place a large piece inside a sieve or colander and pour the liquid through. It is light-textured enough to wrap round soft food such as yogurt cheese (see page 58) to mould it or hold it in shape.

Colanders

2 This well-designed stainless-steel colander has wide grips for lifting or for resting on a bowl, a solid stand, widely spaced holes and an eyelet for hanging. The flat base helps prevent food from being crushed. It is available in diameters ranging from 16 to 28cm. Buy the largest one possible.

3 Although you can set the long-handled colander down, you are more likely to hold it with one hand and the pan from which you are pouring in the other. It is therefore best used for straining manageable amounts rather than the contents of a vast and heavy pot. A diameter of 18–20cm is a useful size to have.

4 The enamelled colander is the kind of utensil you can become inexplicably attached to. Traditional in appearance, it has three sturdy feet to hold it steady, lots of perforations and two U-shaped handles that won't slip or get hot. The enamel may chip in time, but that adds to its charm.

5 Pan drainer Shaped like a crescent moon, the stainless-steel strainer drains small-to-medium amounts of pasta or vegetables directly from the pan. It is held in place by a rim that attaches to the pan edge, and will fit a range of pan sizes.

6 Perforated spoon This vital utensil simultaneously strains and lifts small amounts of food from pans. Cooking juices, water or fat drains off through the perforations.

7 Tea strainer Made of stainless steel, this smart little strainer has a very fine mesh for straining freshly brewed tea or coffee. The wire ear and handle allow you to rest it on your cup – useful if you need two hands to lift a large teapot.

8 Conical strainer This coarse-meshed strainer is handy for straining into a small or narrow container such as a gravy boat or sauce jug. It is available in four diameters ranging from 8 to 20cm.

9 Perforated skimmer The extra-wide, flat bowl skims froth and skin formed by impurities from the surface of stews and stocks. The skimmer can also be used for lifting and draining dumplings, gnocchi or quenelles from broth.

10 Wire skimmer This skimmer is designed for removing fried food from deep fat. The wires allow fat and small bits of sediment to quickly drain away.

12 Wire shaker Charming though it may be, there is no avoiding the fact that water sprays everywhere when you whirl this shaker round. Shaking it gently over the sink does not do the job effectively, and it is best used in the garden.

13 Salad spinner This superbly designed spinner is effortless to use. Unlike many other models, you don't have to cradle it in your arm – just place it on the work surface and pull the string. Centrifugal force presses the leaves against the internal meshed basket, driving water off into the outer container. The clear perspex outer container is smart enough to use as a salad bowl – once you've emptied out the water. There is a more expensive version with a stainless steel bowl.

11 Noodle/pasta scoop This simply designed wire strainer has a pleasingly deep and generous bowl that is ideal for scooping up and straining gnocchi, dumplings and stuffed pasta or noodles such as ravioli, wontons or pot stickers.

yogurt cheese

This is a type of soft cheese popular in the Middle East and India. Yogurt is tied up in cheesecloth and left to strain for 6–36 hours – the shorter time making for a very soft, mild cheese and the longer a denser cheese with a more pronounced flavour. The end result is similar to cream cheese, but lighter in texture and lower in fat.

Yogurt cheese is wonderfully versatile, and combines well with either sweet or savoury ingredients. For a tasty snack, spread it on crackers or toast, or, if it is quite soft, serve it as a dip with crisp vegetable sticks. For a quick and simple dessert, sweeten yogurt cheese with a dusting of sugar or a slick of honey, fruit purée or syrup.

Mixing yogurt cheese with chopped fresh herbs is also delicious. Finely chopped spring onions, green chili, or a little grated ginger can be mixed in, too. Firm yogurt cheese can be shaped into balls or logs and then rolled in sesame seeds, or coarsely ground black or green peppercorns. Serve with flat bread and olives.

basic yogurt cheese

The type of yogurt used will affect the flavour, texture and amount of cheese produced. Plain yogurt gives off a fair amount of liquid, so the weight of cheese produced is less than you would get from thicker set yogurt. Greek yogurt is thicker still, giving off correspondingly less liquid. Bio yogurt is naturally mild in flavour, and produces a mild-tasting cheese, whereas cheese made from yogurt high in lactic acid has a sharp, acidic flavour. Organic wholemilk yogurt makes a particularly delicious cheese – mild in flavour, with a slightly grainy texture.

Enough for 3–4 servings

Tools	Ingredients
three 50cm squares cheesecloth	1kg plain yogurt
colander	
string	
large deep bowl	
wooden spoon	

1 Moisten three squares of cheesecloth and use to line a colander, draping the corners over the sides.

2 Spoon the yogurt into the centre of the cheesecloth. Gather up the four corners and twist to squeeze the yogurt into a ball.

3 Tie tightly with string and fasten onto the handle of a wooden spoon. Rest the spoon over a deep bowl so the yogurt hangs free (or over a shallower bowl, with supports on either side, as here). Make sure there is a gap of at least 5cm between the bottom of the cheesecloth and the base of the bowl. Leave in a cool place to drip for 6–36 hours.

yogurt cheese
with pomegranates, spiced sugar and pistachios

In this simple but exquisite dessert, jewel-like pomegranate seeds and a sprinkling of green pistachios adorn a sweetly perfumed mound of yogurt cheese. The yogurt should be quite soft and mild, so drain it for about 12 hours. You will need around 350g when drained.

Serves 4

Tools	Ingredients
small bowl	6 tbsp pistachio nuts
cook's knife	I quantity yogurt cheese made
wooden spoon	with organic wholemilk yogurt
paring knife	and drained for about 12 hours
	(see opposite)
	¹/₂ tsp rose water
	3 tbsp spiced sugar (see below)
	I large pomegranate

1 Put the pistachio nuts in a small bowl and cover with boiling water. Leave for 5 minutes, then slip off the skins. Chop the nuts roughly and set aside.

2 Beat the yogurt cheese with the rose water and spiced sugar. Divide the mixture between four serving bowls.

3 With a small sharp knife, cut the pomegranate skin lengthways into four segments, taking care not to puncture the juicy seeds inside. Break the pomegranate in half, and then into quarters. Bend the skin back to release the seeds, discarding any bits of membrane. Sprinkle the seeds over the yogurt and top with the pistachios.

Spiced sugar Using a pestle and mortar, grind to a powder 6 cloves, ¹/₂ teaspoon of peppercorns, seeds from 15 green cardamom pods and ¹/₂ teaspoon of fennel seeds. Mix with ¹/₂ teaspoon ground cinnamon. Stir the spices into 350g sugar, mixing well. Keep it in a screwtop jar and use as needed.

pumpkin and girolle soup

This recipe was contributed by the dazzlingly inventive Alain Ducasse, the only chef with six Michelin stars, and mentor to a new generation of chefs who are changing the face of French cooking. A fine-meshed chinois sieve is used to purée the pumpkin for this delicious soup, which is ladled over tiny sautéed girolle mushrooms and topped with crisp lardons and whipped cream.

Serves 4

Tools	Ingredients
cook's knife	3 tbsp olive oil
large saucepan	450g fresh pumpkin, peeled, seeded and cubed
wooden spoon	
chinois sieve and wooden pestle	1 small onion, finely chopped
	450ml chicken stock (see page 62)
deep bowl	6 tbsp unsalted butter
paring knife	$1/2$ tsp fine sea salt, or to taste
mezzaluna	$1/4$ tsp freshly ground black pepper, or to taste
medium frying pan	
utility knife	100ml double cream, lightly whipped until it just forms peaks
small saucepan	
small strainer	100ml double cream, whipped until it holds firm peaks (optional)
small frying pan	*For the garnish:*
paper towels	1 tbsp olive oil
medium saucepan	225g small girolle mushrooms, trimmed and cleaned
balloon whisk	
electric mixer	1 shallot, finely chopped
	2 tbsp unsalted butter
	2 tbsp finely chopped chives
	75g slab bacon or pancetta, cut into 1cm cubes (lardons)
	4 leafy sprigs fresh chervil

1 In a large saucepan, heat the oil over medium-high heat. Add the pumpkin and onion, and stir to coat with oil. Reduce the heat to medium-low and cook until the pumpkin softens and the onions are translucent, about 5 minutes. Pour in enough stock to cover, and cook until the pumpkin is very soft, 10–15 minutes.

2 Remove from the heat and let cool slightly. Set a chinois sieve over a deep bowl, then pour the soup into the sieve, pressing the vegetables through the mesh with a wooden pestle. Reserve the sieved liquid.

3 To prepare the garnish, heat the oil in a medium frying pan over medium heat. Stir in the girolles and shallot and cook, stirring often, until the mushrooms give off their liquid and it evaporates. Add the 2 tablespoons of butter, then the chives. Stir in and remove from the heat.

4 Put the lardons in a small saucepan and cover with cold water. Bring to the boil over high heat, reduce the heat to medium-low, and simmer for 1 minute to blanch and remove some of the salt. Drain and rinse briefly in cold water. Drain again and pat the lardons dry. Sauté the lardons in a small frying pan until they are brown and crisp. Transfer to paper towels to drain.

5 To finish the soup, combine the pumpkin mixture with the remaining chicken stock in a medium saucepan. Bring to a gentle boil, then stir in the 6 tablespoons of butter, and the salt, pepper and lightly whipped cream.

6 Pour the mixture into the bowl of an electric mixer and beat on medium speed until smooth and creamy. Adjust the seasoning to taste.

7 Pour into a warmed soup tureen. Divide the girolle mixture among four warmed soup plates. Spoon in the pumpkin soup. Sprinkle on the lardons, then, if you wish, place a dollop of thickly whipped cream in the centre of each serving. Garnish with sprigs of chervil and serve immediately.

ramen with pork and vegetables

This hearty noodle soup was contributed by leading Japanese food writer Emi Kazuko. Ramen are Chinese-style noodles served in soup with various toppings. The dish is one of the most popular in Japan, where there is a ramen museum, a ramen village, and even ramen appreciation clubs. These noodles can be bought from healthfood shops and good supermarkets. You will need strainers of various sizes for straining the vegetables, meat and noodles.

Serves 4

Tools	Ingredients
medium frying pan	*For the braised pork:*
paring knife	200g pork fillet in one piece
medium saucepan	1 tbsp vegetable oil
small and medium strainers	500ml chicken stock
	5 tbsp shoyu (Japanese soy sauce)
cook's knife	
small bowl	2 tbsp sugar
utility knife	1/2 tsp salt
large saucepan	2 spring onions, sliced into 5cm pieces
colander	
	3–4cm square piece fresh ginger root, roughly sliced
	For the ramen:
	100g spinach, trimmed
	60g bean sprouts
	salt and freshly ground black pepper
	200g dried ramen (Japanese noodles)
	1 litre chicken stock
	1/2 pork or beef stock cube (optional)
	100g baby sweetcorn, cooked
	1 spring onion, finely chopped, to garnish
	rayu, or chilli oil (optional)

1 Brown the pork on all sides in the oil over medium-high heat to seal the meat. Remove from the heat.
2 Put all the other ingredients for the braised pork in a medium saucepan and bring to the boil. Add the browned meat and simmer, covered, for about 1 hour. Leave the meat to cool in the liquid.
3 Lightly boil the spinach, then drain under cold running water for a few seconds. (This makes the green colour bright.) Squeeze out excess water with your hands, and chop into bite-sized pieces.
4 Place the bean sprouts in a bowl and pour boiling water over them. Leave for 5 minutes, then drain. Season with a pinch of salt and pepper.
5 Remove the pork from the saucepan and thinly slice. Drain the cooking juices and reserve, discarding the other ingredients.
6 Cook the ramen in a large pan of boiling water according to the packet instructions. Drain under cold running water to rinse off the starch.
7 Heat the chicken stock, adding the 1/2 stock cube if a stronger soup is required. Stir until the cube has dissolved.
8 Warm up the sweetcorn in boiling water and drain.
9 Put 2 tablespoons of the cooking juices into each of four individual noodle bowls. Add the hot stock to half-fill the bowls. Put a quarter each of the ramen, sliced pork, bean sprouts, spinach and sweetcorn on top. Sprinkle with chopped spring onion and serve hot with rayu.

meat stock

Strainers and skimmers are vital for successful stockmaking. They remove fat, solid matter and impurities, resulting in a clear, sediment-free stock. For a brown stock, brown the bones first in a hot oven, pouring off any fat before adding them to the stockpot.

Makes about 2.3 litres

Tools	Ingredients
cook's knife	About 3 kg beef or veal bones
stockpot	
skimmer or perforated spoon	2 large onions, chopped
	2 large carrots, chopped
colander	2 celery sticks, chopped
large piece cheesecloth	200g mushrooms, sliced
	300ml dry white wine
	1 bouquet garni, fresh or dried
	1/2 tsp black peppercorns

1 Put all the ingredients in a stockpot. Add 10 litres of cold water (a) and bring to the boil. Don't add salt at this stage – it's better to add it to the dish in which the stock will be used.

2 As the liquid reaches boiling point, a harmless scum forms. Scoop this off with a skimmer or perforated spoon and discard (b). Turn the heat to a simmer and continue to skim off the scum. Cook, uncovered, for up to an hour until the mixture has reduced by at least half.

3 Remove the pan from the heat and let the stock stand for 30 minutes. This allows debris to settle.

4 Line a colander with wet cheesecloth. Slowly pour the stock through the cloth, leaving the debris behind (c). For a clearer stock, pour the liquid through the cloth again. Cool the stock, then chill. Scrape off any fat that forms on the surface.

chicken stock

This gelatinous stock forms part of the 'pumpkin and girolle soup' recipe contributed by Alain Ducasse (see page 60). The stock differs from others in that the chicken carcasses are brought to the boil quickly, then boiled for 5 minutes, during which time the scum is removed – most recipes specify that this stage is carried out slowly. After rapid boiling, the carcasses are drained and returned to the pan with fresh water, and the usual slow simmering begins. This method certainly speeds things up, and the finished stock is delicious.

Makes about 2 litres

Tools	Ingredients
cook's knife	About 3kg raw chicken carcasses and/or parts
vegetable peeler	
stockpot	2 onions, quartered
skimmer or perforated spoon	1 large leek, green parts only, rinsed well and cut into 5cm pieces
strainer or colander	1 carrot, halved
large piece cheesecloth or butter muslin	2 celery stalks, cut into 5cm pieces
large bowl	1 tomato, quartered
	6 parsley stems
	1 tbsp coarse sea salt
	1 tsp black peppercorns

1 Place the chicken in a large stockpot. Cover with cold water and bring to the boil over high heat. Boil for 5 minutes, skimming the surface frequently.

2 Drain the chicken and rinse under cold water. Rinse out the stockpot to remove the scum, return the chicken to the pot, and cover with cold water.

3 Add the vegetables, parsley stems, salt and peppercorns, and bring to the boil over high heat. Reduce the heat and cook, uncovered, at the barest simmer for 2 hours, without stirring or skimming. Remove from the heat and let cool briefly.

4 Strain the stock through a strainer or colander lined with cheesecloth or muslin, into a large bowl. Let the stock cool completely, then store, covered, in the refrigerator for no more than 24 hours, or freeze in small containers.

5 Before using, scrape off and discard the fat that forms on the surface.

boiling
and
steaming

pots and pans

Along with knives, pots and pans can be your pride and joy, for it is within them that your efforts at chopping, slicing, mixing, measuring and seasoning culminate, and the alchemy that is cooking takes place. Because of this, pots and pans are more complex than knives. Knives are about cutting and the results are instant and obvious. Pots and pans require patience and co-operation. You have less control over the way they behave, and for successful results, you must get to know how they react with different ingredients and heat levels.

My earliest pots and pans were mean-spirited affairs made of thin aluminium or coated with quaintly speckled enamel. I did not treat them well, nor they me. However, though they warped and buckled, burnt me and the food, they did not succeed in dampening my embryonic passion for cooking. Since then I have amassed a collection, and the more I cook, the better quality I buy.

There's no denying that good pots and pans are expensive. As with knives, it's worth starting off with three or four good ones that earn their keep, rather than buying several of inferior quality. There is a growing number of so-called 'chef's sets' on the market, but don't be tempted by them. You will inevitably end up with pans you never use because you don't cook the type of food for which they are intended. They also take up valuable storage space. You may of course be given a set of pans, perhaps as a wedding present, but this leaves you the problem of having to live up to their demands. If you are new to cooking, you may feel pressured into embarking on recipes that are over ambitious or simply not your style. It is far better to build up your collection of pans gradually and let your culinary repertoire expand at its own pace.

I Non-stick aluminium saucepan Sturdily built but not too heavy, this pan is made from non-warping cast aluminium, coated inside and out with a SilverStone® non-stick surface. This makes for fat-free cooking and easy cleaning, so it is a good pan for sauces, porridge, scrambled eggs and other foods that stick. Suitable for all hobs except the induction type, the pan has a thick ground base for fast, even heat distribution. The oven-proof glass lid has a heat-resistant knob. This pan is available in blue, green or black, and in three sizes, from 1.1 litres to 2.25 litres.

2 Stainless-steel saucepans These sleek, professional pans are made in top-grade 18/10 stainless steel (see 'material choice', page 8). The base has an aluminium/magnetic steel/aluminium core sealed between two layers of stainless steel. This means the pans are suitable for all hobs, including the induction type, which is activated by magnetism. The handles are welded to the body of the pan over a large area so cannot come loose. They are comfortable to hold but tend to get hot when cooking at high temperatures. Despite this minor drawback, these pans are a joy to use. They are available in five sizes, from 1 litre to 4.8 litres, and it's well worth having all five; otherwise aim for the largest, the smallest and one in the middle.

Choosing saucepans

Before buying, think carefully about how you will use and store your saucepans. Size, shape, weight and material (see 'material choice', page 8) are all-important.

A basic set of saucepans might consist of a couple of smallish pans, say 1.7–2 litres, one or two medium pans (3–4 litres) and a large pan (5 litres). A very small pan (1 litre) is useful for melting butter, boiling eggs or reheating small amounts of food, and a small non-stick milk pan is a must for heating milk.

The base should be thick and solid – a thin base will buckle over high heat, making it useless on a sealed cooking plate. The base of a good-quality pan is ground flat as opposed to stamped flat; check for the marks of the grinding machine. Test for flatness by placing the pan on a level surface and pressing to see if it wobbles.

If your hob has radiant rings, measure the rings and buy pans to fit. The perfect pan should fit exactly over the heating element. This keeps the heat where it is meant to be – under the pan.

A pouring lip will cope with a thin liquid like milk, but not a thick sauce or soup. If the pan is to be used by a left hander, you will need a left-handed pan or one with two pouring lips or a continuous pouring rim that lets you pour from any point. A pouring rim also pours large amounts of liquid and thick liquids more efficiently.

Handles should be long enough to distance your hand from the heat. They must be comfortable to hold and firmly attached to the pan. Rivets or a firm weld are better than screws. Pans that hold 3 litres or more should have two handles – either a pair of ears, or one ear opposite a long handle. Lid handles and knobs should be heat-resistant. If metal, it should conduct heat less well than the pan. If your pan is intended to go in the oven, the knob and handle need to be heatproof. Lids are essential for steaming, poaching and stewing, and for bringing water to the boil sooner. They should fit snugly, especially if you want to use the pan for steaming.

Material science

The two basic properties required of a material used for pan making are that the surface is non-reactive, so it will not taint the food, and that it conducts heat efficiently and evenly. As no single material meets these requirements, manufacturers use combinations of metals. For example, the base may be made from a layer of aluminium or copper (both chemically reactive but excellent conductors of heat) sandwiched between stainless steel (a poor conductor of heat but non-reactive to chemicals). Another solution is to coat the inside of the pan, and sometimes the outside too, with a non-reactive substance such as vitreous enamel, or to treat it electrolytically by anodizing, as in anodized aluminium. Anodizing hardens aluminium and makes it non-reactive.

3 Anodized aluminium saucepans These hard-anodized pans are not cheap but they are guaranteed for life. The base is heavy and solid, and the smart grey anodized coating will not chip, peel or scratch when scrubbed.

The cast stainless-steel handles are triple riveted to the body and stay cool in use. The larger sizes of pan have a helper handle opposite the long one so you can lift it with both hands. They are available in four sizes, from 1.4 litres to 4.3 litres.

4 Anodized aluminium milk pan As boiling milk tends to stick to the pan, this is one of the few saucepans that needs a non-stick surface. This one, in heavy-gauge aluminium, has an anodized surface on the exterior and a hard-wearing, easy-to-clean, non-stick interior. The stainless-steel handle is firmly riveted. If you are left handed, make sure your pan has a pouring lip on both sides.

beyond basics

As your cooking skills develop and you gain in confidence, you will undoubtedly start to yearn for more pots and pans. The ones shown here are the next step up from a basic set and will ease tasks such as preserving and making soups and sauces. Buy them according to need. Some of these pans are quite large, which

1 Stockpot with pasta insert If you care about good soup, a stockpot is almost a basic requirement. This large stainless-steel pot accommodates several kilos of meat, bones and vegetables. The tall, somewhat narrow shape slows evaporation of liquid and allows solid matter to remain submerged for hours at a time, while coaxing out delicious flavours. A five-layer ground base (see 3 Double boiler) permits prolonged simmering without scorching. The generously sized and firmly welded U-shaped handles make for safe lifting.

The perforated pasta insert lifts out easily, leaving the cooking water behind – a process that is easier and safer than carrying a heavy pot from hob to sink. Those who wear glasses will also appreciate steam-free lenses. The insert doubles up as a strainer when blanching vegetables.

2 Pressure cooker Pressure cookers work by trapping steam by means of a specially designed tight-fitting lid. As pressure builds up, the temperature rises above boiling point and steam is forced into the food, reducing cooking time and cutting down on fuel.

This stainless-steel model has a domed lid housing a self-regulating valve, which limits the amount of escaping steam. Normal cooking time is reduced by at least one third. The solid ground base is suitable for all hobs, including the induction type.

3 Double boiler/casserole This stainless-steel pan has a well-fitting lid and a solid, five-layer base – a core of silver alloy/copper/silver alloy is sandwiched between two layers of stainless steel, giving excellent heat conduction.

Simmering water in the lower pan gently heats the base of the upper one without touching it. This is an infallible way of making egg-based sauces such as hollandaise – the gentle heat keeps egg proteins from coagulating, as they do in scrambled eggs, so they are able to emulsify with butter to form a smooth and silky sauce.

Used either on its own or with the lid, the bottom part of this pan doubles as a saucepan or casserole.

4 Copper saucepan A copper pan is the Rolls Royce of cookware. This splendid saucepan encapsulates the properties of three different metals: copper for speedy and even conduction of heat, a taint-free stainless-steel lining – far more durable than traditional tin – and a stay-cool, cast-iron handle. The only drawback is that once you have one copper pan, you'll want more.

might be off-putting if you have limited storage space. However, because they can perform two or three functions, they may actually help you to economize on space as well as money. For example, a large stockpot is well worth having as it can double up as a pasta pot and, even though it does not have the flaring sides that help evaporation, as a preserving pan. A pressure cooker without its lid makes a very useful large saucepan.

5 Preserving pan This capacious, 13-litre, stainless-steel cauldron will satisfy the needs of the most dedicated jam-maker. It has a solid ground, wide base to ensure even heat distribution, and gently flaring sides that increase the surface area and encourage evaporation. The invaluable helper handle assists with lifting and pouring, while the semi-circular handle across the top can be locked in an upright position to keep the pan cooler.

6 Slant-sided aluminium saucepan Made from heavy-gauge aluminium with a 6mm ground base, this homely-looking pan is perfect for sauces. The narrow base speeds up boiling, and the splayed-out sides increase the surface area, encouraging evaporation and reduction of liquids. A continuous turned edge means you can pour from any position without messy drips. The bakelite handle remains cool during cooking. It is best not used for cooking vegetables as uncoated aluminium will cause them to discolour.

8 Bain marie Any saucepan can be turned into a double boiler with this 'universal' stainless-steel bain marie. Place it in the top of the pan above simmering water and it will heat the contents gently and evenly. This is an ideal way of making egg-based sauces and custards, melting chocolate or cheese, or reheating leftovers without scorching them.

9 Butter warmer This neat little stainless-steel pan, measuring just 11cm in diameter, is specially designed for warming or clarifying small amounts of butter. It is attractive enough to be brought to the table, for example to pour butter over asparagus. You can also use it for warming brandy or melting chocolate. It has just one pouring lip, so left-handers either have to pour 'backwards' or use their right hand.

7 Slant-sided anodized aluminium saucepan
Altogether smarter with its grey anodized coating and elegant stainless-steel handle, this 1-litre pan is similar in design and function to the uncoated aluminium pan. Use it for reducing sauces, making gravy or warming hot chocolate. Two pouring spouts make it suitable for left or right handers. It is also available in a 2.3-litre size, which makes a brilliant sauté pan. The larger size has a continuous turned rim instead of pouring lips, making it easier to tip out solids and liquids.

Blanching This is a method of partially cooking vegetables by immersing them briefly in rapidly boiling water. Vegetables that are to be frozen are blanched to halt enzyme activity. It is a method used by chefs to cook vegetables ahead of serving – they can be quickly reheated with no loss of flavour or texture. After blanching, vegetables are best plunged into a bowl of iced water, a process known as 'refreshing'. This also has the effect of heightening the colour, especially of green vegetables.

Reducing You can make quick gravy to serve with pan-fried meats, such as chops or steak, cooked in a sauté pan. After cooking, remove the meat to a serving dish and keep warm. Add a small glass of wine to the pan juices and stir well, scraping up any meaty deposits with a wooden spoon or wooden spatula. Boil rapidly to reduce by a third, then pour in 2–3 tablespoons of cream or crème fraîche. Allow the gravy to bubble for a few seconds, add seasoning and pour over the meat.

Simmering Cooking a casserole or stew at a simmer, with the occasional bubble breaking the surface, helps soften the collagen in meat tissues, making tough meat more tender. The process is further helped by adding acid ingredients such as tomatoes and wine. A casserole dish with a heavy metal base allows for gentle simmering.

Gentle boiling The turbulent action of fast boiling can break up the texture of certain foods, such as floury potatoes, as the starch swells. When boiling point is reached, turn the heat to a gentle boil. Some starchy foods can boil over if the heat is too high, for example pasta and rice. A tablespoon of oil helps to maintain surface tension.

specialist pans

These pans are marvellous to have for those times when you get the urge to whip up zabaglione or boil caramel, for example. Though they tend to be expensive, it is a pleasure to use pans in which form so closely follows function. The rounded shape of the zabaglione pan perfectly echoes the shape of the whisk used to create the foam. The fondue pot is wide and shallow enough for several people to dip their forks at once without being overcrowded. The flared sides of the polenta pan increase the surface area and encourage evaporation.

1 Polenta pan Known as a 'paiolo' in Italy, this beautiful copper pan makes the rather arduous process of stirring polenta a pleasure rather than a chore. The pot heats quickly and evenly, while flared sides make prolonged stirring easier. The shapely wooden handle stays cool and comfortable during stirring. The pan is unlined and should therefore be rubbed with vinegar and salt before and after each use (see 'Meringues', page 49).

2 Zabaglione pan This solid copper pan is designed to froth up the warm, creamy alcoholic custard known as 'zabaglione' in Italy and 'sabayon' in France. Set over a low flame or double boiler, the copper conducts even, gentle heat, which softly coagulates the egg proteins as you whisk. The deep, rounded bowl facilitates the rapid scooping movement needed to create the foam.

3 Sugar boiler This attractive copper pan is ingeniously designed to cope with the very high temperatures produced during sugar boiling. The pan is unlined because the traditional tin lining would melt (see 'material choice', page 8), and sugar does not react adversely with copper. You might expect the handle to be made of wood, which remains cool, but at the temperatures reached wood might catch fire. Even oven gloves are in danger of igniting. The problem is solved by the hollow copper handle, into which chefs traditionally insert a length of broomstick. Because the handle is funnel shaped, the wood is in contact with only a small area of hot metal, so the wood does not catch fire and it prevents heat from being conducted to the end where your hand is.

4 Saucier Normally found only in the professional kitchen, this saucier is made from best-quality 18/10 stainless steel (see 'material choice', page 8). It has an inner core of aluminium, not just in the base but all the way up the sides, for optimum heat conductivity. The pan can be used on all hobs, including the magnetic induction type.

The rounded, slightly flared sides facilitate easy stirring and whisking, and restrict splattering. The pan is perfect for reducing liquids, as well as browning meat and sautéing vegetables. It comes in four sizes, from .9 litre to 5 litres.

5 Cheese-fondue pot A traditional cheese fondue consists of cheese and wine melted together in a pot over a flame. Diners spear chunks of bread on forks and swirl them in the communal pot, which is known as a 'caquelon' in France and Switzerland. As high temperatures make cooked cheese stringy, cheese-fondue pots are traditionally made of glazed earthenware, which withstands only gentle heat. Meat-fondue pots are made of metal. Popular in the seventies, and a ubiquitous item on the wedding-present list, fondue sets seem to be making a comeback.

basic polenta

Polenta is a mild-tasting grain with a deeply satisfying flavour. Cooked to a porridge-like consistency it can be served wet, like mashed potato, or cooled and cut into shapes, then grilled or fried until crisp – delicious for mopping up tasty juices and gravy.

Polenta is traditionally made in a special pan (see page 69), but a large, heavy-based saucepan makes a good substitute. The hot mixture plops enthusiastically as it cooks, so use a long-handled wooden spoon to avoid being scalded.

Tools

polenta pan or large, heavy-based saucepan
long-handled wooden spoon
wooden board or wide, shallow pan
palette knife

Ingredients

1.5 litres water
1 tsp salt
300g polenta

a

b

c

d

1 Bring the water and salt to a boil in a polenta pan or large saucepan, then turn down to a medium simmer. Stirring with one hand, use the other to add the polenta in a steady stream, holding your fist in a funnel shape (a).

2 Continue to add the polenta, making sure each fistful is absorbed before adding another. Traditionally, polenta is stirred in one direction only (b).

3 Polenta is best stirred for up to 20 minutes. Take care as the hot mixture will spurt upwards as it thickens. It is cooked when it comes away from the side of the pan (c).

4 To serve polenta wet, simply spoon it into a serving dish. Otherwise, pour it onto a board or a wide, shallow pan, level the top with a wet palette knife and allow to set firm before frying or grilling (d).

grilled polenta with mushrooms, celeriac and sage

This recipe uses polenta that is slightly stiffer than the basic mix, and is particularly suitable for cutting into shapes before frying and grilling. Use two or three different kinds of cultivated or wild mushrooms such as chanterelles, oyster, shiitake, chestnut or portobello.

Serves 4–6 as a starter or light meal

Tools	Ingredients
polenta pan or large, heavy-based saucepan	500ml water
	1/2 tsp salt
long-handled wooden spoon	125g polenta
18cm-square roasting pan	2 tbsp olive oil, plus extra for brushing polenta
palette knife	
cook's knife	2 tbsp butter
grill pan	2 tbsp chopped fresh sage
pastry brush	100g peeled celeriac, cut into 1–5cm cubes
vegetable peeler	
small frying pan	500g assorted mushrooms, cut into bite-sized chunks if large
tongs	
large frying pan	2 garlic cloves, finely chopped
	1 tbsp chopped flat-leaf parsley
	squeeze of lemon juice
	pinch of cayenne pepper
	sea salt and freshly ground black pepper
	small sage sprigs, to garnish

1 Cook the polenta following steps 1–3 of 'basic polenta' (see opposite). Pour the polenta into a small, square roasting pan and level the surface with a wet palette knife. Leave to cool.

2 Preheat the grill to very hot. Meanwhile, slice the polenta into six rectangles, then halve each rectangle diagonally to make two triangles. Brush both sides with olive oil, and spread out in a grill pan.

3 Heat 1 tablespoon each of the oil and butter in a small frying pan. Add half the sage and gently fry for a few seconds to flavour the oil. Add the celeriac cubes and fry over medium heat for a few minutes, turning them with tongs until lightly coloured on all sides. Remove the pan from the heat and set aside.

4 Heat another tablespoon of butter and oil in a large frying pan. Fry the remaining sage for a few seconds, then throw in the mushrooms. Stir-fry over moderately high heat for 7–9 minutes until most, but not all, of the liquid has evaporated. Add a little more oil if necessary.

5 While the mushrooms are cooking, grill the polenta pieces until golden and crisp at the edges, then turn them over and grill the other side.

6 Keeping an eye on the polenta, tip the contents of the celeriac pan into the mushrooms, and add the garlic. Fry for another minute, then add the parsley, lemon juice and seasonings.

7 Divide the polenta triangles between individual plates and pile the mushroom mixture on top. Garnish with the sage sprigs.

coffee...

Coffee-making at its most basic is simply a matter of pouring boiling or near-boiling water over fresh grounds and allowing them to steep. However, during nine centuries of coffee-drinking, brewing equipment has proliferated. Despite the choice, there is no best way to brew coffee, though aficionados will swear by a particular method. Whether you like to kick-start the day with a blast of espresso or prefer something mild and milky, the best way is how you like to make it.

1 Drip-filter coffee maker This electric coffee maker has a convenient swing-out filter holder operated by a press button, a front-filling water tank and a magnified water-level indicator.

To use a drip-filter machine, fill the cone-shaped filter with finely ground coffee, and then with boiling water, which filters through into the carafe. The cone shape permits fast saturation of the grounds, while the density of the filter slows down the rate at which water passes through. The filter also absorbs some of the coffee's natural oils, resulting in a brew that is light and clear but somewhat lacking in body.

2 Percolator Something of a museum piece, this device forces boiling water up through a hollow central shaft and showers it over the coffee grounds suspended at the top of the shaft in a perforated container. The water drips back to the bottom of the pot, via the container, and thus continually boils and circulates until the indicator light shows the coffee is ready. The device produces a somewhat 'stewed' brew that nevertheless has its fans.

Espresso coffee makers
4 This traditional aluminium machine can be used on the stove top. Fill the bottom container with water, insert the funnel-shaped filter and fill it with medium-ground coffee. Then screw the top section to the lower. Once heated, water and steam are forced through the grounds and on through a narrow shaft in the top container. A high-octane brew then gushes out of the top of the shaft, filling the upper container. It is available in 3-, 6-, 9- and 12-cup sizes.
5 The 'designer' espresso maker works in a similar way, except the coffee shoots into the cup through a down-turned shaft. It comes in 1- and 2-cup sizes.

6 Plunge-filter coffee maker
This provides one of the simplest ways of making a rich brew. Pour boiling water over coarsely ground coffee in the base of the glass beaker. After five minutes of steeping, press the plunger – two filter discs attached to a central shaft – down over the grounds. This traps them in the base of the beaker and leaves the coffee ready to pour. When buying, make sure the discs fit tightly into the beaker, or grounds will escape up the side. One drawback is that the coffee does not maintain its temperature while steeping. This can be overcome by using an insulated cover; newer models have an acrylic outer casing, which retains heat better.

3 Cappuccino creamer To create the essential froth for your cappuccino, half-fill the creamer with milk, heat until it is almost boiling, then put on the lid and pump the plunger for about 30 seconds. Alternatively, you can heat milk in a saucepan and froth it with a spiral whisk.

... and tea

Like coffee, properly made tea needs clean-tasting, freshly drawn and boiled water. A kettle is essential – even though water boils equally well in a saucepan, it is simply not the same. Water is more easily poured from a kettle's spout, and because the water is enclosed, it boils more quickly and uses less fuel.

There was a time when a kettle was simply a kettle; nowadays there is a choice of designs. If you are choosing a kettle to use on the hob, look for one with a broad, flat base to maximize contact with the heat source and speed up boiling. The handle should be positioned well above the lid, and the spout should direct steam away from your hand. If you want an electric kettle, bear in mind that the tall jug type needs less water to cover the heating element, so it boils more quickly and uses less electricity than the traditionally shaped sort. Some are fitted with a fine mesh filter just behind the spout to separate out the sediment that may accumulate in hard-water areas.

There is no doubt that tea is better made from loose leaves that are allowed a five-minute steep in a teapot, rather than from a teabag pressed hurriedly into a cup. Like kettles, teapots come in a range of styles, materials, colours and shapes. Tea seems to taste better when made in a glazed china or earthenware pot. Glass and stainless-steel pots also work well but are more expensive.

Whatever the material, there are three main features to look for: a non-drip spout, a lid that stays in place as you pour the last cup, and a handle large enough to distance your knuckles from the pot.

1 Whistling kettle The Alessi Kettle with Bird, designed in 1985, has become something of a modern design icon. It fulfils all the essential requirements of a stove-top kettle, possessing a wide, thick base, a comfortable, heatproof handle that positions your hand away from the steam, and a cheerful whistle.

2 Cordless kettle Clean, pristine and almost surgical in appearance, this electric kettle has no trailing cord and is good-looking enough to be used in the smartest of surroundings. A see-through indicator enables you to measure the amount of water and prevents over-filling.

3 Traditional kettle This homely looking kettle is made in enamelled steel and comes in a range of bright colours, as well as black or white. The handle and knob are heat resistant. The solid ground base is suitable for all types of hob, including the induction type and the solid heating plates of range cookers.

4 China teapot This classic white porcelain teapot has a pleasingly fat spout, a round knob for lifting the lid and a capacious, curved handle. An integral filter prevents stray tea leaves from escaping into your cup.

5 Glass teapot/ tea press This elegant teapot works in the same way as a plunge-filter coffee maker. Tea leaves are held in a perforated container while steeping. When the tea looks the right colour, press down the plunger and remove the central insert.

poachers and steamers

Poaching and steaming are beautifully simple methods of allowing clean, natural flavours to shine through. In fact, steamed food can make a welcome change from a surfeit of chargrilling, searing and stir-frying. If you're on a low-fat diet, steamed food is definitely worth trying, and if you cook in cramped conditions or are without an oven, steaming food in tiered containers can be a lifesaver, as the Chinese have known for centuries.

Poaching is a technique that falls midway between boiling and steaming. Foods such as chicken or fish are laid on a rack in a pan with just enough liquid to cover the bottom, and simmered very gently until they are barely cooked. The food remains wonderfully moist and, because it has not been subjected to vigorous boiling, keeps its shape.

As the name suggests, steaming is a method of cooking food in the vapours that rise from boiling cooking liquid, which may be water, stock or wine. Virtually any food can be steamed: meat, poultry, seafood or vegetables. It is mainly the Asian cuisines – Thai, Japanese and Chinese – that make the most of the techique. Food is placed on a plate or in a perforated container set above the liquid and covered with a lid to keep the steam in. Because the food is not in direct contact with the liquid, fewer nutrients are lost by leaching. If the liquid is water, it will be nicely flavoured by the food being steamed, and can be used to make a gravy or sauce, or for cooking rice.

If you have never tried steaming, start off with a 'universal' steamer insert, or a fold-out steamer. Then you can progress to a more expensive multi-tiered set. Some items, such as fish kettles or asparagus steamers, are expensive and worth buying only if you are likely to use them regularly. On the other hand, a Christmas pudding ball costs little and is fun to have even if you use it only once a year.

2 Three-piece steamer You can cook a complete meal with this 20cm diameter, tiered steamer set. Made of top-quality 18/10 stainless steel, the bottom pan has a thick ground base for maximum heat conduction and for use on any hob, including the induction type. The bottom pan can be used to simmer a stew, while large vegetables such as cauliflower or root vegetables steam in the deep middle container, and smaller vegetables steam in the top. The lid fits all three parts so you can use the base alone or with one steamer basket only.

1 Couscousier This two-tiered aluminium pot is designed for cooking the North African semolina-based dish couscous. The lower pot stews meat, poultry or vegetables in a fragrant broth, from which steam rises through the upper pot's perforated base to cook the couscous above.

3 Bamboo steamers Pleasing and inexpensive, these Chinese steamers can be used for a variety of foods, such as whole fish, pieces of poultry, vegetables or dumplings. They come in various sizes and can be stacked as high as you like in a wok or pan of boiling water. New steamers should be soaked for 15 minutes to get rid of the pervasive smell of bamboo.

5 Steamer trivet This classic design has not changed much since the days of Mrs Beeton. The trivet sits in the bottom of a pan of simmering water and raises a smaller pan or basin off the surface, creating a makeshift bain marie. The grooved surface helps to prevent pans from slipping off the stand. It can also be used as a trivet to protect the work surface from hot pans.

6 Christmas pudding steamer This solid steamer is perfect for making a traditional round Christmas pudding. A cluster of perforations at the top lets the steam escape. Suspend the steamer from the handle of a wooden spoon resting on opposite sides of the pan.

7 Fold-out steamer Suitable for most saucepans, this compact stainless-steel steamer opens out like the petals of a flower. The perforations and gaps between the overlapping petals allow steam to penetrate well and the feet raise the food above the boiling water. The central stalk limits the ways in which you can arrange the food, but on some models the stalk is removable. The fold-out steamer is available in two sizes, expanding from 14cm to 22.5cm, and from 17.5cm to 27.5cm.

4 Rice steamer Save on cleaning the pan and cook rice in a perforated rice steamer. The perforations are small enough to prevent uncooked grains of rice escaping. It is important not to overfill the steamer as rice doubles in volume once cooked. The chain has a hook on the end so you can hang it from the side of the pan.

8 Asparagus steamer Some cooks think that if asparagus stalks are cooked until tender, the tips will be overcooked. This tall, narrow steamer allows the stalks to stand upright in boiling water while the tips cook in the steam. However, if you don't mind stalks a little on the crunchy side, you could just lay the spears flat in an ordinary steamer.

9 Fish kettle/poacher Small or medium-sized fish can be poached in any pan into which a rack will fit, but large, round fish such as salmon need an elongated pan that allows the fish to lie flat. The fish is placed on a perforated, two-handled rack that lifts easily from the pan, draining the fish without spoiling its shape. Some fish kettles are so large they will straddle two burners. There is also a glamorous diamond-shaped kettle that is designed especially for poaching flat fish such as halibut and turbot.

10 Egg poacher Though it is not a poacher in the strict sense, as the eggs are cooked by steam, this magnificent pan not only cooks faultless eggs but, without the insert, doubles up as a non-stick sauté pan. Made in top-quality 18/10 stainless steel (see 'material choice', page 8), the poacher has non-stick, removable egg cups, and a 5mm thick, encapsulated base suitable for all types of hob.

11 'Universal' steamer insert Sit the stepped base of this perforated container in any of your saucepans, and you have an instant steamer for cooking vegetables, fish, meat or poultry. It is an indispensable utensil.

tunisian couscous with greens, red peppers and garlic

The recipe for this traditional Tunisian dish was contributed by Paula Wolfert, the award-winning American food writer whose speciality is Mediterranean and Middle Eastern cuisine. The melange of dill, fennel and celery leaves, red-pepper flakes, and spices makes for a light and delicious couscous, which Paula suggests serving with glasses of buttermilk, as is the custom. If you don't have an authentic North African couscousier (see page 74), use a large saucepan with a tightly fitting steamer insert. If fennel leaves are hard to find, increase the amount of dill. Tabil is a Tunisian spice paste, which you can buy from shops specializing in Middle Eastern Food.

Serves 6

Tools

cook's knife or mezzaluna

garlic press

paring knife

couscousier or large saucepan with steamer insert

large frying pan

wooden spoon or turner

long fork

tongs

Ingredients

3 tbsp chopped dill leaves

3 tbsp chopped fennel leaves

6 tbsp chopped flat-leaf parsley

handful of celery leaves, chopped

handful of carrot tops, chopped

1 large spring onion, thinly sliced

1/2 small leek, thinly sliced

8 tbsp olive oil

1 small onion, chopped

3 tbsp tomato paste

5 large garlic cloves, crushed

2 tsp sweet paprika

2 tsp salt, or more, to taste

2 tsp ground coriander or tabil

1 tsp ground caraway seeds

1 1/2–2 tsp dried red-pepper flakes, preferably Aleppo, Turkish or Near East pepper for best flavour

450ml water

450g medium-grain couscous

1 fresh green chilli, stemmed, deseeded and finely chopped

1 red pepper, stemmed, deseeded and cut into 6 pieces

6 garlic cloves, peeled and left whole

1 Fill the bottom of the couscousier or saucepan with water and bring to the boil. Put the perforated top or steamer insert in place. Add all the green leaves, spring onions and leeks, and steam, covered, for 30 minutes (a).

2 Remove from the heat and allow to cool, uncovered. When cool enough to handle, squeeze out the excess moisture and set aside.

3 Heat the oil in a large frying pan and add the onion. Gently fry for 2–3 minutes to soften, then add the tomato paste. Cook, stirring, until the paste glistens.

4 Add the crushed garlic, paprika, salt, coriander or tabil, caraway and red-pepper flakes. Cook slowly until the mixture is well blended. Add 225ml water, cover and cook for 15 minutes.

5 Remove the pan from the heat. Stir the dry couscous into the contents of the pan and stir until well blended (b). Stir in the steamed greens, leeks and spring onions, and mix well. Fold in the green chilli, pieces of red pepper and garlic cloves.

6 Top up the bottom of the couscousier or saucepan with water and bring to the boil. Put the top or steamer insert in place. Add the contents of the pan and steam, covered, for 30 minutes (c).

7 Turn out the couscous onto a large, warm, serving dish. Use a long fork to break up any lumps. Use tongs to fish out the whole garlic cloves and pieces of red pepper, reserving them.

8 Stir 125ml water into the couscous, taste for seasoning and cover with foil. Set in a low oven for 10 minutes before serving.

9 When ready to serve, decorate the couscous with the slices of red pepper and whole garlic cloves. Serve with glasses of buttermilk.

steamed salmon with ginger, spring onions and bok choy

Steamed on a trivet over a wok, this comforting and easily digested dish is ideal if you are under stress or entertaining in a hurry. It needs nothing more than a simple accompaniment of plainly boiled white rice. Make sure the fish is very fresh.

Serves 4

Tools	Ingredients
paring knife	4 salmon steaks or cutlets, each about 2.5cm thick
23cm heatproof plate	2 tsp finely chopped fresh ginger root
trivet	
aluminium foil	2 tbsp rice wine or dry sherry
wok with lid	1 tbsp soy sauce
another wok or large, heavy-based frying pan	½ tsp salt
	4 tbsp groundnut oil
fish turner	2 large salad onions, green parts included, shredded, but with green and white parts kept separate
small saucepan	
	3 heads bok choy, quartered lengthways
	good squeeze of lime juice
	coarsely ground black pepper
	2 tsp sesame oil

1 Rinse the fish steaks, pat dry with paper towels and place in a single layer on a heatproof plate.

2 Combine the ginger root, rice wine or dry sherry, soy sauce and salt. Sprinkle this over the fish, rub it into the flesh and leave for 20 minutes, turning once.

3 Place a trivet in a wok and add enough water to reach halfway up the trivet. Bring to the boil, place the plate of fish on the trivet and cover with a loose tent of foil. Adjust the heat so the water is just boiling and put the lid on the wok. Steam for 10–15 minutes until the fish is opaque and just starting to flake.

4 While the fish is steaming, heat 2 tablespoons of groundnut oil in a second wok or large, heavy-based frying pan. When the oil is almost smoking, fry the white part of the salad onions for 30 seconds. Throw in the bok choy and stir-fry for 4–5 minutes until the stalks are just tender, but still crunchy. Splash with a good squeeze of lime. Arrange in small mounds on four warmed serving plates.

Steaming in a wok You will need a metal or wooden trivet (see page 75) and a domed lid, often sold with a wok set. Food is steamed on a heatproof plate set on the trivet in the base of the wok. If you like, you can wrap food such as small chicken breasts or fish steaks in greaseproof paper parcels, as shown. Alternatively, bamboo baskets (see page 74) can be stacked on the trivet; they can also be used on a trivet in an ordinary saucepan.

5 Using a fish turner, carefully lift the fish pieces from the wok and place on top of the bok choy. Arrange the green salad onions on top and sprinkle with several grindings of black pepper.

6 Heat the sesame oil and remaining 2 tablespoons of groundnut oil in a small saucepan. When it is very hot, pour over the green salad onions and fish. Serve immediately.

frying
and
grilling

frying pans

Using a frying pan of the right shape, size and material makes a marked difference to the cooking process and your finished dish. There is an enormous choice and a good pan is not cheap, so before buying think carefully about the type of food you cook and the type of hob you cook on.

Different-shaped pans suit different tasks: high-sided pans help prevent splattering; rounded, outward-sloping sides comfortably accommodate spoons and spatulas, making stirring easier; shallow sides help you to deftly slide the contents out of the pan. Size is equally important. Small amounts of food cooked in too large a pan will dry and burn; juices will spread too thinly and evaporate. On the other hand, if you crowd food into a pan, it will steam and stew instead of browning and crisping.

1 Round frying pan The outwardly sloping sides allow you to slide a spatula in and out of the pan with ease, while a wide diameter provides generous food-to-heat contact. It is made of warp-free cast aluminium with a superior Silverstone® non-stick coating and stainless-steel handle.

2 Wok Designed for continuous movement over high heat, the wok's conical shape tips food continually back to the centre, where the heat is at its most intense. Because the food is constantly on the move during stir-frying, much less oil is needed, making it a healthy option. Round-bottomed woks are suitable for gas hobs; a slightly flattened bottom works better on ceramic or electric hobs. This one has wooden handles, which remain cool despite the intense heat generated from the wok.

3 Ridged, square frying pan Falling midway between a frying pan and a stovetop grill, this pan has a ridged base that lifts food clear of fat and gives appetizing stripes to steaks and chops. From the same range as the round pan (1), it is made of cast aluminium with a durable non-stick coating.

4 Stainless-steel sauté pan Made from superior 18/10 stainless steel (see 'material choice', page 8), this pan has a thick ground base for maximum heat contact. A wide diameter and high, straight sides allow quick, light frying of chicken quarters or large amounts of potatoes in relatively little fat. The high sides also prevent spattering or spilling as food is turned and shaken. Once the food is evenly browned, the pan can be partly or fully covered, enabling the contents to cook at a more gentle pace.

Which metal?
To fry food, it must be heated quickly and evenly, so the best pans are made of heavy-gauge metals that are efficient conductors of heat (see 'material choice', page 8). Copper pans lined with tin or stainless steel are superb, but they are also very expensive. Anodized cast aluminium is one of the best materials as long as it is medium to heavy gauge; lightweight pans tend to buckle and develop hot spots. Stainless steel looks stunning and is easy to clean, but used alone, does not conduct heat well. Combined with a thick layer of copper or aluminium, however, it is hard to beat.

Cast iron is heavy and initially slow to heat, but once hot it maintains its temperature and conducts heat evenly. A small cast-iron frying pan is handy for dry-frying whole spices, but before buying a larger one, check that you can manage the weight – especially if you have weak wrists.

Heavy-gauge, untreated, mild steel is another option. It needs seasoning with oil and in time it builds up a heavy patina that makes the surface non-stick. Until then it needs careful treatment to prevent rusting. Untreated steel pans should never be washed, but simply wiped clean and oiled.

Non-stick pans have improved greatly in recent years, and are worth having not only because they are easy to clean, but also because there is something delectable about the way morsels of food slide around the pan, sizzling in their own tasty juices rather than a bath of oil. A non-stick frying pan not only enables you to cut down on fat, but also allows you to really taste the food.

Choosing frying pans
For a basic set, choose two or three round, heavy-based frying pans for general use: one with a 25–28cm diameter base, another with a 20–23cm base and possibly a third with an 18cm base – invaluable for a solitary fry-up. You might also consider buying a large, high-sided sauté pan with a lid for poultry quarters or chunky potatoes. A smallish sloping-sided pan is essential for omelettes or crêpes. If you like stir-fries, you will also need a wok, though a heavy-based frying pan makes a reasonable alternative.

When buying a new pan, check the handle is firmly welded or riveted. If the pan is very big, an ear-shaped helper handle opposite the long one makes lifting safer. Some handles are cast in one piece with the pan. Though less likely to work loose, integral handles tend to become hotter than handles that are attached separately.

5 Splatter screen Frying causes splattering and spitting of fat, especially if moist food is added to hot oil (always pat food dry before frying). When placed over the pan, this fine-meshed screen keeps fat where it belongs.

6 Hard-anodized aluminium stir-fry pan Invaluable for a solo stir-fry, this 20cm pan has a unique, long-lasting, non-stick surface that is covered with minute ridges. The flat bottom is suitable for all hobs.

7 Steel omelette pan Smooth sloping sides and a flat bottom ease the deft manoeuvres necessary for making a perfect omelette. Made from untreated steel (see 'Which metal?', above), this pan deserves respect – use it only for frying omelettes or crêpes and treat it with care.

8 Hard-anodized aluminium chef's pan This invaluable pan can be used as a wok or, with its heat-toughened glass lid, as a casserole. It has a heavy ground base for maximum heat conduction, a durable non-stick interior and two stainless-steel handles for easy lifting.

beyond basics

These pans are tailor-made for a particular use. Some are expensive, and they all take up valuable storage space. Consider them only if you regularly cook, or plan to cook, the food for which they are intended. On the other hand, if you were to buy an oval fish fryer, you might eat fish more often, which is no bad thing; and the chestnut pan would be lovely to have at Christmas....

I Crêpe/pancake pan Made of heavy-gauge aluminium with a hard-wearing Silverstone® non-stick surface, this pan will have you tossing pancakes like a pro. The smooth 25cm base allows batter to spread evenly and thinly as you rotate the pan, and the shallow sides facilitate flipping.

2 Oval pan This excellent heavy-gauge pan is just right for frying two or three plump fish to crisp perfection. The non-stick surface allows minimal fat to be used and prevents fish skins sticking to the pan. It can be cleaned in seconds.

3 Fajita pan This oval pan is designed for sizzling the cut of beef (skirt steak, resembling a 'fajo' or belt) after which the dish was named. Made from hard-anodized aluminium, the pan rapidly reaches the high temperature needed. Widely flaring, shallow sides permit quick and easy turning and serving.

4 Blini pan From the same professional range as the crêpe pan, this neat 12cm pan has smooth, rounded sides that encourage yeast-leavened batter to rise. The handle is long enough to distance your hand from the heat.

5 Danish cake pan With its seven rounded depressions, this hefty lump of cast iron cooks to perfection Danish 'aebleskiver' (apple dumplings). Cast iron conducts and maintains the level of heat necessary for cooking the dumplings right to the centre.

6 Karhai (Indian wok) As versatile as a Chinese wok, the karhai is used for frying or, with its lid in place, for slowly simmering meat, poultry, seafood and pulse dishes. Made of heavy-gauge carbon steel with a Xylan® non-stick surface, the karhai has up-tilting handles that enable you to carry it to the table.

8 Chestnut pan More of a roaster than a fryer, this broad, shallow pan is designed for toasting chestnuts over a gas flame or open fire. The wide perforations allow the skins to remain in contact with the flames and char, while the nut meat inside remains succulent. There is no better way to pass a winter evening.

7 Paella pan This capacious pan is designed to accommodate the wealth of ingredients that go into a paella. Made of fast-heating, hard-anodized aluminium, the pan has rounded, flaring sides for easy sautéing of chicken, chorizo and seafood, and for stirring in rice. The thick ground base and ridged, non-stick surface prevents burning and sticking, while the magnificent domed stainless steel lid encourages steam to condense and keep the food moist. The pan has the customary two handles (instead of one long one) with which to carry it safely to the table.

scallop and shiitake stir-fry

Contributed by Raymond Blanc, acknowledged as one of the world's finest chefs, this recipe reflects his insistence on fresh, top-quality produce and light, unmasked flavours. The stir-fry is a wonderful mixture of sweet and bitter, soft and crunchy. It is cooked in a non-stick chef's pan (see page 81), which, as Raymond says, 'epitomizes where we are in our cooking today. It has a good design, weight and excellent heat conduction. It's the best non-stick pan I've ever used; I adore the glass lid as I like to see what's going on inside the pan.'

Serves 4 as a starter or light meal

Tools	Ingredients
preparation bowls	12 large scallops and their corals
cook's knife	2 tbsp sesame oil
paring knife	3 tbsp groundnut oil
citrus juicer	200g small shiitake mushrooms
large non-stick chef's pan or wok	2 heads baby bok choy, leaves left whole, stalks sliced
long-handled wooden spoon or wok ladle	into 2cm pieces
	150g sugar-snap peas, sliced in half lengthways
	3cm piece fresh ginger root, finely chopped
	2 garlic cloves, finely chopped
	juice of 1 unsprayed lime
	salt and freshly ground black pepper

1 Cut each scallop in half and each coral into three pieces.
2 Heat a high-sided pan or wok with the two oils, add the scallops and corals, and toss for a minute over your highest heat.
3 Add the mushrooms, sliced bok choy stalks and sugar-snap peas, then stir-fry for a further minute.
4 Spoon in the ginger and garlic, along with the bok choy leaves and a little water, and stir-fry all together for another minute or two until the leaves have wilted.
5 Add the lime juice, season to taste, then serve on four large, warmed plates.
Variations Monkfish makes a wonderful substitute for the scallops, and if you can't find bok choy, use Chinese cabbage, choi-sum or spinach. If shiitake mushrooms are not to your liking, any mushroom can be used instead.

chicken in a red-pepper sauce

The recipe for this colourful chicken dish was contributed by Madhur Jaffrey, best-selling author and authority on Indian food. The dish is cooked from start to finish in a karhai (see page 83) – a versatile pan similar to a Chinese wok, and perfect for stir-frying, deep-frying and leisurely braising.

Serves 4

Tools	Ingredients
cook's knife	1/2 large onion, coarsely chopped
paring knife	2.5cm cube fresh ginger root, coarsely chopped
blender or food processor	3 garlic cloves
rubber or plastic spatula	25g blanched, slivered almonds
karhai or wok with a lid	2 red peppers, deseeded and coarsely chopped
citrus juicer	1 tbsp ground cumin
	2 tsp ground coriander
	1/2 tsp ground turmeric
	1/8–1/2 tsp cayenne pepper
	2 tsp salt
	7 tbsp vegetable oil, such as sunflower or grapeseed
	1kg chicken pieces, skinned and cut into small serving pieces
	150–250ml water
	2 tbsp lemon juice
	1/2 tsp coarsely ground black pepper
	fresh coriander leaves, to garnish

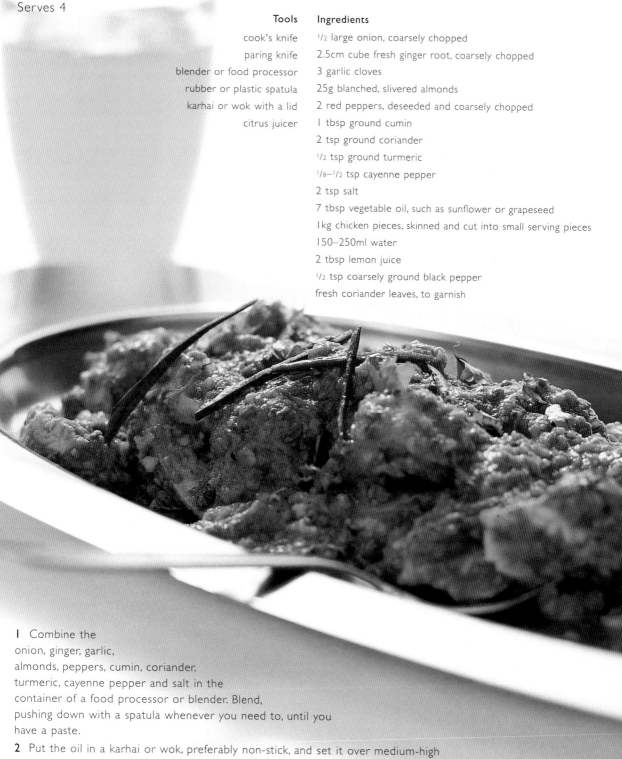

1 Combine the onion, ginger, garlic, almonds, peppers, cumin, coriander, turmeric, cayenne pepper and salt in the container of a food processor or blender. Blend, pushing down with a spatula whenever you need to, until you have a paste.

2 Put the oil in a karhai or wok, preferably non-stick, and set it over medium-high heat. When hot, pour in all the paste. Stir and fry it for 10–12 minutes or until you can see the oil forming tiny bubbles around it.

3 Add the chicken with 150ml water, the lemon juice and the black pepper. Stir to mix in and bring to the boil. Cover, turn the heat to low and simmer gently for 25 minutes, stirring occasionally, until the chicken is tender. Add a little more water if necessary.

4 Serve straight from the karhai or transfer to a serving dish. Garnish with coriander leaves before serving.

total immersion

The equipment featured here is designed for deep-frying food in boiling fat. An enormous variety of foods, both sweet and savoury, is cooked in this way – batter-coated fish, chips, fritters, meat balls, Spanish churros, Middle Eastern falafel and kibbeh, Asian rice balls and crispy noodles, Indian pakoras and sweets, to name more than a few.

Because so many different foods can be deep fried, it is important that the cooking vessel does not absorb odours and is reasonably easy to clean. And as success depends on frying at the correct temperature, the material from which the pan is made must be able to conduct heat evenly and maintain its temperature. Most important of all, because a large quantity of boiling fat is an obvious hazard, the equipment must be safe to use.

I Tempura pan This beautiful, heavy, iron pan is the secret to making faultlessly crisp tempura and other deep-fried foods. It transfers heat quickly and evenly, and keeps the oil at a stable 170°–180°C. The pan has a spout for pouring off oil, and a rack for draining and keeping morsels of food warm. It comes with a pair of chopsticks for cooking.

2

I

3

2 Chip pan Made from high-quality enamelled steel, this pan will not absorb smells or grease, and is easy to clean. It conducts heat well, and can be used on any hob, including the induction type. Fat drains easily from the inner wire basket, the handles of which have extensions that rest on the outer handles and lift the food clear of the fat below. The pan can also be used for blanching vegetables.

3 Potato nest fryers Finely shredded potatoes or other starchy foods are fried in the outer basket, while the smaller basket presses the contents into a nest shape. The inner basket is hinged to the outer one at the bowl end, and the two are held in place by a ring that fits over both handles. The handles are long enough to protect your hand from the heat of the fat.

4 Electric deep fryer This sensibly shaped deep fryer makes efficient use of storage space and allows you to deep-fry a whole fish without bending it. Like all electric fryers, this one is thermostatically controlled, but unlike most others, it filters cooking scraps into a cold zone between the heating element and the bottom of the pan. This ensures the oil stays clean and fresh for longer. With the exception of the heating element, all components can be put in a dishwasher. The fryer is supplied with a lid.

4

Deep-frying Successful deep-frying depends on so many variables that it could rightly be called an art rather than a technique. The type, condition and temperature of the oil, type and size of pan, the moisture content of the food, its porosity and surface area, the cooking time – all of these affect the quality of the finished product.

The type of fat or oil is critical. All fats and oils decompose once they reach a certain temperature – some may even spontaneously ignite. Once you can see and smell smoky fumes, or the fat becomes darker or flecked with particles, decomposition is under way. The point at which this happens is called 'the smoke point'. Butter and all animal fats have a low smoke point (about 190°C), which is why they quickly burn when overheated. Vegetable oils have a higher smoke point (about 230°C); groundnut oil has one of the highest, which makes it the most suitable oil for deep-frying and stir-frying.

If you don't have a thermometer, you can check the temperature of the oil by dropping a small cube of bread into it. When the bread browns in 1 minute, the oil is ready to use.

The issue of whether oil can be reused is a contentious one. Although some cooks condone it, I would never do so, as successful deep-frying depends on getting the oil good and hot. Once oil has been heated to a high temperature, decomposition takes place rapidly and the flavour becomes tainted. If you do re-use oil, make sure you don't overheat it and that it is thoroughly strained after use.

Chips
1 After cutting, soak the raw chips in cold water for 30 minutes to remove excess starch. Drain and pat dry. Fill the fryer about a third full of groundnut or sunflower oil. Heat the oil to 160°C. Place a good handful of raw chips in a wire basket and deep-fry them for 5 minutes, until a pale golden colour.
2 Drain and increase the oil temperature to 190°C. Refry the chips for about a minute, until golden and crisp. Drain well and season.

Churros
3 Traditional Spanish churros are made with a choux paste piped directly into hot groundnut or sunflower oil using a 1cm fluted nozzle. Fry at 180°C for 2–3 minutes until golden brown and crisp. Toss in caster sugar and serve. Great served at breakfast, dipped into hot chocolate or coffee.

Tempura
4 To make Japanese tempura, dip thinly sliced vegetables or large peeled prawns into a lightly mixed batter of 2 egg yolks, 275ml water and 200g plain flour. Deep-fry two or three pieces at a time in groundnut or sunflower oil at 180°C, in a tempura pan or wok. Remove the cooked tempura and place on the special rack to drain.

The direct heat of the grill quickly seals succulent juices beneath a crisp exterior, and creates unique, intense flavours.

5 Flat stove-top grill This beautifully designed oval pan is made of stylish matt black cast iron. It has an integral handle and a low-rimmed edge that allows easy access and turning of food. Designed for hob-to-table use, the pan comes with its own heatproof stand, made of hard-wearing rubberwood.

6 Circular wire rack Used on the stove top, this non-stick rack is handy for grilling chillies, peppers, onion rings and other fresh vegetables, and for heating flat breads and tortillas. The wooden handles remain cool during use. It measures 25.5cm in diameter.

7 Flat griddle This 30cm anodized aluminium griddle can be used to grill traditional drop scones and griddle cakes and appetizing toasted sandwiches. It will also quickly cook eggs and bacon. The hooped handle packs flat for storage.

8 Waffle iron This attractive metal mould, known as a 'gauffrier' in France, has two hinged and embossed plates, between which waffle batter is cooked over a source of heat. The handles are held together by a clip to prevent the batter from leaking out, and are long enough to protect your hands from the heat. Hand-operated waffle irons date back to the fifteenth century; some of them were real masterpieces, embossed with intricate patterns, coats of arms or magical or religious symbols.

9 Ridged stove-top grill pan Made of vitrified cast iron, this shallow, rectangular grill pan has a ridged surface that produces appetizing brown stripes and raises the food slightly to prevent it from sitting in fat. A continuous gutter and a wide pouring lip allow fat to be drained off easily. The steel-wire handle folds over the pan for convenient storage.

grilled squid with chillies

Ruth Rogers and Rose Gray have made London's River Café one of the world's most acclaimed restaurants. In their recipe a cast-iron stove-top grill cooks squid in seconds.

Serves 6

Tools	Ingredients
cook's knife	6 medium squid
serrated knife	4–6 mild red chillies, deseeded and finely chopped
paring knife	extra-virgin olive oil
small whisk	sea salt and freshly ground black pepper
stove-top grill, lightly oiled	2 tbsp lemon juice
	225g rocket leaves
tongs	3 lemons, quartered, to serve

1 Slit the squid open and scrape out the guts, keeping the tentacles in bunches. Remove the eyes and mouths.

2 Using a serrated knife, score the inside of the squid bodies with parallel lines. Then do the same in the other direction.

3 Put the chillies in a bowl and cover with about 2.5cm of oil. Season to taste.

4 To make the dressing, combine 6 tablespoons of olive oil with the lemon juice. Season to taste and whisk until smooth.

5 Place the squid (including tentacles) scored-side down on a hot stove-top grill and season. Grill for 1–2 minutes then turn them; they will instantly curl up, by which time they will be cooked.

6 Put a squid on each plate with some rocket, tossed in the dressing. Place a little chilli on the squid and serve with the lemon quarters.

grilling

Grilling is a method of cooking by direct, dry heat, either under the radiant heat of the grill or directly over the heat of the hob or barbecue. Cooking must be fast enough to simultaneously seal in juices and produce a crisp crust.

Grilling is not nearly as simple as it sounds – how many of us have been confronted with chicken that is blackened on the outside and raw within? Successful grilling calls for tender, succulent ingredients, an intense source of heat, and, for grilling on the stovetop, pans that heat up fast and can withstand high temperatures without warping.

For cooking under the grill, you will need a heavy-gauge metal pan with a rack. The one that came with your oven might be adequate, but if it has warped or twisted, it is worth replacing. Ovenproof baking dishes (see pages 108–109) can also be used under the grill, and are ideal if you want to form a crust or melt a cheese topping on an almost-cooked dish.

For stovetop grilling, you will need a thick, flat, cast-iron pan or griddle, with or without ridges. A rectangle or a long oval is the most practical shape as you can load more food onto it. As an alternative to the flat grill pan, there are cast-iron pans with shallow, raised sides that look like frying pans, but are much heavier.

1 Toaster Though you can toast bread under the grill, an electric toaster does the job more quickly and cheaply. This slim stainless-steel model toasts four slices at once. It does not have the usual pop-up mechanism – the bread is put into a wire holder and removed manually when done.

2 Salamander Rather like a branding iron, the small iron disc is heated until it is red hot, then used for browning or caramelizing the surface of individual dishes, particularly crème brûlée. Although the same effect can be achieved with a grill, the salamander heats the surface of the food only, so you can enjoy the sensuous contrast of chilled, soft custard and hot, crunchy caramel.

3 Blow torch The vogue for blackened and seared food that started in the eighties has seen the blowtorch migrate from the workshop to the kitchen. It is a useful tool for skinning peppers and tomatoes, caramelizing sugar, searing meat, or just adding that extra touch of black to finished dishes. This sleek black model has push-button ignition and an easily adjustable flame.

4 Reversible grill This cattleman-sized (52.5 x 24cm) cast-iron grill is designed for use across two burners or on the barbecue. The ridged side sizzles steaks, chops, burgers, fish or vegetables with a minimum of fat. Use the smooth side for potato rösti, traditional drop scones, or for a large batch of grilled sandwiches. Both sides of the grill have a gutter for channelling away unwanted fat.

fired up

The choice of barbecue equipment grows each year. Before buying, it is vital to do some research and to consider the practicalities. As well as space, location and storage issues, think about how many people you are likely to cook for. If a barbecue is too small the grill will become congested and food won't cook properly; if it's too big, you will waste fuel. For four to six people you need a grilling area at least 30 x 30cm, or 35cm in diameter.

Charcoal is by far the best fuel. Though they are convenient to use, gas and electric barbecues do not impart the same flavour. In any case, lighting, fanning, watching and waiting are essential parts of the ritual. Choose irregularly shaped lumpwood charcoal rather than briquettes. It ignites easily, burns at a fierce heat and gives off a pleasing aroma. Scattering rosemary twigs on the coals once the food is cooking adds to the fragrance. Avoid instant-lighting charcoal or lighting agents unless you want the food to taste of petrol.

All charcoal barbecues are made up of two components: a firebox that holds fuel and a rack that holds food. Many models include a grate to allow air to circulate under the fuel, and some have vents for regulating heat. Rack height is usually adjustable for controlling the cooking temperature.

1

1 Long-handled utensils Tools with extra-long handles allow you to baste, spear and turn while distancing your hands from the heat. The tongs are well sprung and have a ridged surface for efficient gripping. The slotted turner has a cleverly angled edge to prevent food from accidentally slipping off it. The brush allows you to safely anoint food with oil or a marinade without fear of drips and flare-up.

4

4 Disposable barbecue Hardly atmospheric but great for a spur-of-the-moment picnic, disposable barbecues are usually ready to use in 15–20 minutes, and will often keep going for up to two hours. They are good for a couple of steaks or chops, or several sausages.

2 Oval portable barbecue This rugged cast-iron barbecue is well suited to outdoor cooking. The rack can be set at two levels and is sturdy enough to support a pan, so can be used for boiling and simmering as well as grilling. A damper regulates heat and the flip-down lid allows you to add more fuel.

2

5 Wire holders Turning whole items of food is made easier with these specially shaped wire holders. Brush with oil first to prevent sticking.

3

3 Hibachi barbecue Originally from Japan, these neat cast-iron barbecues are weighty but still portable. They have short legs and can be set on the ground if you don't mind squatting, or placed at table height on a fireproof surface. The fuel sits in a trough close to the rack, the height of which is adjustable. Though convenient and easy to use, hibachis have a small firebed so the fire doesn't last long. They are best used for small pieces of quick-cooking food.

5

Choosing a barbecue

Barbecuing at its most basic requires no more than a cake rack set on two bricks. For many years this is what I used, and all I could afford; the results were delectable, or so they seemed at the time. Equally simple, but tidier, is a disposable barbecue, which consists of a heavy foil tray, firelighter, fuel and a rack. All you need is a match.

Cast-iron portable barbecues, such as the hibachi, are hard-wearing and easy to use. They have short legs and can be used on the ground or on a heat-resistant surface at table-top height.

The food that can be cooked on small portable barbecues is of necessity rather restricted. If you aspire to cooking a whole fish or a spit-roasted chicken, you will need to invest in a more sophisticated piece of equipment. The free-standing brazier types have an open grill and sometimes come with a wind shield, hood and/or spit-roaster. They are fitted with wheels or detachable legs, and some models are portable, making them convenient to transport to a picnic. Make sure the legs are long enough for you to be able to cook comfortably; it is less back-breaking to squat on the ground than to be half bent over something that is not quite the right height for standing at.

The bulbous kettle barbecues have a domed lid that excludes air, thus reducing the risk of flare-up. The lid also deflects heat onto the food, resulting in quicker and more even cooking, and enabling larger pieces to be cooked with success. Though the rack on kettle barbecues is not adjustable, the firebox has vents that enable you to control the cooking temperature. An enamelled finish is more durable than the heat-resistant paint that some models are treated with.

The pedestal or pillar types of barbecue have a firebed set above an integral flue. The flue is filled with newspaper, which is lit through a ventilation hole, preferably with a long match. The upward draught creates a powerful draw that quickly lights the fuel.

6

7

6 Pedestal barbecue This sleek, stainless-steel model is good-looking enough to grace the balcony of the most design-conscious loft dweller. No need for messy chopped kindling, just stuff the flue with yesterday's newspaper and ignite. Billowing smoke may initially annoy the neighbours, but it soon dies down. The barbecue has ventilation holes for regulating temperature, and a windshield with three slots for adjusting rack height. Drawbacks: the outer surface becomes intensely hot and is therefore a hazard to children and pets; the barbecue is tall and the base relatively narrow, so it must be set on very flat, level ground to remain stable.

7 Kettle barbecue An all-American classic, this outstanding barbecue is made in rust-resisting enamelled steel, and has a thermometer in its lid for accurate monitoring of temperature. The vents open for cooking while the lid is lowered, creating convection heat that produces a tasty crisp exterior and seals in juices. A touch of a button conveniently releases ashes into a container below the firebox.

Successful barbecuing

O If possible, line the base of the firebox with silver foil and cover with sand. This absorbs fat drippings and helps prevent flare-up.

O Light the barbecue with good old-fashioned paper and sticks. Once lit, leave the charcoal alone until it is covered in pale grey ash. Only then is it ready to use.

O To assess temperature, hold your palm 15cm from the grill and count. If you can feel the heat after 2–3 seconds, the fire is hot enough for cooking small thin items such as chipolata sausages, skewered food and fish fillets.

O If you can hold your hand over the grill for 4–5 seconds, the heat is suitable for larger pieces that need longer cooking such as spare ribs, chops or chicken quarters

O If you can withstand the heat for longer than 5 seconds, the fire is not hot enough.

O Keep tools with extra-long handles within easy reach of the barbecue. You will need tongs, a fork, a spatula and a brush. A pointed knife is useful to test for doneness.

O Keep one pair of tongs solely for transferring raw meat and poultry to the barbecue. This will reduce the risk of food poisoning.

barbecued seafood skewers
with sun-dried tomato basil aïoli and grilled vegetable salad

Perfect for a summer lunch, this mouthwatering recipe was contributed by Wolfgang Puck, one of an influential breed of chefs who launched new trends in Californian cuisine with an expert blend of fresh local ingredients and classical French technique. Cook the vegetables first, then stoke up the barbecue so it is very hot before you grill the seafood.

Serves 6–8

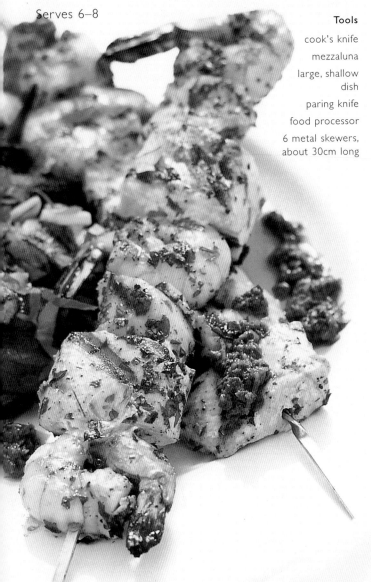

Tools

cook's knife
mezzaluna
large, shallow dish
paring knife
food processor
6 metal skewers, about 30cm long

Ingredients

450g swordfish or salmon, cut into 2.5cm cubes

450g scallops, halved if large

450g large, uncooked prawns, shelled and deveined

salt

For the marinade:

7 tbsp olive oil

2 tbsp freshly ground black pepper

4 tbsp finely chopped herbs, including basil, oregano, thyme and parsley

For the sun-dried tomato basil aïoli:

75g sun-dried tomatoes, packed in oil

2 tbsp chopped basil

8 garlic cloves, or 1 head, roasted

2 tbsp balsamic vinegar

7 tbsp extra-virgin olive oil

salt and freshly ground black pepper

For the grilled vegetable salad:

225g spring onions or leeks, halved lengthways

225g small carrots or sweetcorn, halved lengthways

225g courgettes, halved lengthways

225g Japanese aubergines, halved lengthways

2 red peppers, halved and deseeded

1 head fennel, cut lengthways into 1cm thick slices

4 large tomatoes, halved and deseeded

salt and freshly ground black pepper

225ml olive oil

1 tbsp finely chopped garlic

1 tsp ground cumin

7 tbsp balsamic vinegar

7 tbsp coarsely chopped fresh herbs, including basil, oregano, parsley and thyme

1 Mix all the marinade ingredients together. Put all the seafood in a large shallow dish and pour the marinade over. Refrigerate for 2–4 hours.

2 To make the aïoli, put the sun-dried tomatoes, basil, garlic and balsamic vinegar in a food processor and purée until smooth. With the motor still running, slowly add the olive oil and season with salt and pepper. Refrigerate until ready for use.

3 For the grilled vegetable salad, mix all the vegetables with salt, pepper and 100ml of the olive oil. Place on a hot barbecue and grill until tender and brown (some vegetables may take longer than others). Remove from the grill, cool and cut into 2.5cm pieces. Cut the tomatoes into 1 cm cubes and add to the vegetables. Mix the vegetables with the garlic, cumin, vinegar, herbs and remaining olive oil.

4 When ready to cook the seafood, thread onto skewers, alternating prawns, scallops, and swordfish or salmon (about 175g per skewer). Season each skewer with salt.

5 When the barbecue is very hot, grill the seafood for about 4 minutes on each side.

6 To serve, divide the vegetable salad between individual plates and place a skewer on top of the salad. Drizzle part of the aïoli over the seafood and serve the rest on the side.

slightly smoky grilled quails
with ginger, mirin, basil and sesame

At London's famous Sugar Club restaurant, brilliant New Zealand chef Peter Gordon combines modern British food with the very best of Pacific Rim flavours. His quail recipe is perfect for the barbecue – as he says, 'Quails are great to barbecue because they're easy to hold in your hands, and they'll dribble just the right amount of juice down your chin.' Though not essential, a barbecue with a lid allows the quails to take on a smoky flavour without burning.

Serves 4

Tools	Ingredients
kitchen scissors	8 quails
large bowl	a good handful of basil leaves, plus a little extra, shredded
paring knife	3 tbsp plus 1 tsp sesame oil
long-handled tongs or fork	2 tsp sesame seeds
citrus juicer	thumb-sized piece fresh ginger root, very finely chopped
	3 garlic cloves, finely chopped
	4 tsp Thai fish sauce
	4 tsp mirin
	4 tsp wine vinegar
	1 tbsp demerara sugar
	lime juice, to taste

1 Hold a quail in your hand, breast-side down, and cut out the backbone with a pair of kitchen scissors (see 'spatchcocked poussins', page 26). Put the bird in a large bowl. Repeat with the others.

2 Add the remaining ingredients to the bowl, reserving some of the basil, and toss together. Cover with clingfilm and leave to marinate in the fridge for at least 6 hours. Remove from the fridge about 2 hours before you're ready to cook, so the birds have time to come to room temperature.

3 Once the barbecue coals are glowing, make them into a mound in the centre. Lay the quails, flattened out and breast-side up, on the rack in a ring around this hot mound. Close the lid if you have one, as this will keep some of the heat and the smoke in. Cook for 6 minutes, then open the lid, turn over the quails, close the lid again and cook for another 5–8 minutes.

4 Test a quail by poking its thigh with a sharp knife at the thickest point. If the juices run clear, it's cooked. If they are still pink, continue to cook for a couple more minutes, then test again. If the bird is black and flaming, you'll be going hungry.

5 Transfer the cooked quails to a platter and sprinkle with the extra shredded basil and a squeeze of lime.

tools for lifting and turning

When manoeuvring food at high temperatures, you need long-handled tools to protect your hands. The tools should grip well or be shaped in such a way that they are compatible with the nature of the food and/or the shape of the pan. Hang them within easy reach of the hob so you don't have to fumble in a drawer. Avoid lifters and turners with wooden or painted handles, and those with rivets and joins. A continuous piece of metal is easier to clean and will last a lifetime.

1 Fish lifter This efficient tool enables you to lift a whole fish and keep it intact. The bowed blade has a gently chamfered edge that slips easily under the fish without tearing the skin. The perforations allow fat to drain.

2 Wok turner The rapid stirring, turning and lifting of food that stir-frying demands are made simple with this shovel-shaped tool. It is available with or without perforations.

3 Fish turner A thin, rounded blade allows careful handling of fish and other delicate foods. The slots make the blade flexible and allow fat to drain away as you lift.

4 Spring-action tongs Popular with professional cooks, these stainless-steel tongs have a positive spring action and ample scalloped heads that allow you to clasp food securely.

5 Scissor-action tongs With their inwardly curved, pincer-like heads, these tongs are ideal for lifting and turning small pieces of food. The plastic-coated handles are comfortable to hold and remain cool in use.

6 Angled turner Ergonomically designed for comfort, this angled turner is available in right- and left-handed versions.

7 Non-stick turner Even though non-stick pans are more durable than they used to be, it still makes sense to use a non-stick turner. This one is made of die-cast aluminium and has an angled blade with generous slots for efficient drainage of fat.

8 Bamboo rice paddle and fork These are used for serving rice or mixing it with other ingredients. The paddle's tapered edge separates rice grains without crushing them.

9 Wire scoop This is ideal for scooping up french fries, sauté potatoes and any deep-fried food. Oil quickly drains away through the coarse wire mesh. The scoop also makes a useful skimmer.

10 Turning fork A five-pronged fork delicately harpoons slippery food.

roasting stewing and baking

roasting

Look for good, solid roasting pans and be prepared to pay for them – the one that came with your oven will inevitably warp and you'll end up with the fat gathering in one corner, leaving the rest of the pan high and dry.

Roasting pans come in a variety of materials. However, size and weight are more important. Pans need at least 5cm of space around them for air to circulate, so check the size of your oven before buying. Get several sizes – if you roast a small piece of meat in too large a pan, the juices will spread thinly and burn. Conversely, a large joint or bird in an undersized pan will cook unevenly. Pans should be rigid, with sides high enough to restrict splattering. Sizeable roasts can be heavy, so when choosing a large pan, make sure it has handles or a flat rim you can grip easily. A non-stick surface is worth having if you are trying to reduce your fat intake. If you like roasted vegetables, get a largish shallow-edged pan too. It will double as a baking sheet.

I Double oven gloves All-in-one oven gloves are easier to use, store and find than a pair. The deep pockets are triple-lined on the palm side and double-lined on the back, protecting your hands and wrists even if you happen to brush against the insides of the oven.

3 Anodized aluminium roasting pan This heavy-duty roasting pan and the shallow roasting tray (4) are guaranteed not to twist or buckle when exposed to high temperatures. The hard surface is resistant to scratches, even from metal utensils. The base is solid enough to stand up to the direct heat of the hob, so you can use the pan for gravy-making on top of the stove. The pan is available in a range ofl sizes and will last a lifetime.

4 Lifting forks A pair of lifting forks ease the transfer of meat from roasting pan to serving platter. Choose forks that have at least three prongs. Any fewer and the meat is in danger of dropping between them.

2 Enamelled self-basting roaster This cleverly designed, high-quality roaster has a series of dimples set into the lid. These encourage moisture to gather and drip evenly over the meat, resulting in a particularly succulent roast.

The steel rack lifts the meat out of the fat. Because the meat is completely enclosed, its surface will not become crisp. If you want it to be crisp, remove the lid towards the end of the cooking time.

5 Anodized aluminium roasting tray The ideal pan for roasting vegetables. Sliced aubergines, onion rings and peppers, for example, will become deliciously crisp and sticky as the dry heat of the oven circulates over them, unimpeded by a high-sided pan. The generous surface area means you can give your vegetables plenty of room. If you cram them together they will simply steam in their own juices and remain disappointingly pallid.

6 Fat separators As fat always rises to the top as it cools, a utensil with a spout that joins the jug at the base allows you to draw off liquid, leaving the fat behind. The elegant porcelain fat separator (left) is designed to pour fat-free gravy from a deep spout at one end, and the risen fat from a shallow spout at the other. The more functional-looking acrylic fat separator (right) is available in 1-litre and 360ml sizes, and can be used for gravy, soup or stock.

7 Vertical chicken roaster Cut down on roasting time with this vertical roaster, which is designed to conduct heat directly to the inside of the bird. The bird browns and crisps evenly, while fat and juices drain into the base of the pan.

8 Trussing needle Resembling a giant darning needle with an eye large enough to take a piece of string, a trussing needle makes a more secure job of sealing flaps and openings in poultry or tying a joint into a neat, compact shape. Unlike a skewer, it can pass all the way through the meat, drawing the string with it.

9 Enamelled roasting pan This heavy-duty pan measures 38 x 26cm and is perfect for larger joints. Sturdy handles assist with lifting and fold out of the way so they don't take up space in the oven. A lip in one corner accurately directs fat and juices as you pour them off. The enamelled surface is smooth and easy to clean.

11 Bulb baster Rather surgical in appearance, this glass tube and rubber squeeze ball is used for basting as well as drawing off fat. Fill the tube with meat juices by squeezing the ball, then release and hold the tube upright. The fat will rise to the top and the fat-free juices can be squirted over the meat or used to make a gravy or sauce. Calibrations show exactly how much liquid the tube has sucked up, which can be useful in sauce-making.

10 V-shaped roasting rack Fully adjustable, this rack lifts any size of bird or joint well away from the base of the pan. Ordinary flat racks do little more than raise the meat a centimetre or two above the pan, which is of little use if you are cooking a goose or a duck, for example, as they produce copious amounts of fat. The V-shape not only facilitates clearance of fat but allows air to circulate under the meat, resulting in faster, more even cooking and crisper skins.

12 Stainless-steel mini roasting pan People who live on their own need not deprive themselves of the pleasure of a roast. Just 20cm square, this smart little pan is the perfect size for one. It is also useful for roasting whole onions, beetroot or turnips. Made of top-grade stainless steel, it can also be used under the grill and on the hob.

pork and crackling

Jamie Oliver is one of Britain's most talented young chefs, and this recipe perfectly captures his feisty, no-fuss style. Boneless pork is roasted flat, directly on the bars of the oven shelf, with a roasting pan beneath to catch the juices. This produces succulent meat, the crispest, crunchiest crackling ever, and gravy that will have you licking your plate. Ask your butcher to take the meat off the bone and then to score the skin across in deep lines about 5mm apart. Ask for the bones to be chopped up so you can use them to make the gravy.

Serves 8

Tools	Ingredients
pestle and mortar	1/2 pork loin, roughly 3kg on the bone
large roasting pan	sea salt flakes
medium roasting tray for browning bones	1 tbsp chopped fresh rosemary
aluminium foil	1/2 tbsp fennel seeds
large frying pan or saucepan for making gravy	5 cloves garlic
wooden spoon	8 tbsp balsamic vinegar
sieve	4 bay leaves
	2 tbsp olive oil
	pork bones, chopped
	5 outer celery sticks, roughly chopped
	1 large carrot, roughly chopped
	1 large onion, roughly chopped

1 Rub some salt and rosemary into the pork skin, pushing it into the scored lines.

2 Using a pestle and mortar, smash up the fennel seeds, then the garlic and remaining rosemary. Rub this mixture into the meat – not the skin, or it will burn. Place the meat in a large roasting pan with the balsamic vinegar, bay leaves and olive oil. Leave for about 30 minutes to marinate.

3 Preheat the oven to its highest temperature and brown the bones. Rub the pork skin with more salt.

4 Place the pork directly onto the bars at the top of the oven. Put the browned bones and vegetables in the roasting pan with the left-over balsamic marinade and add 600ml water. Set the pan in the oven directly under the pork, so that as the pork cooks, all the goodness drips from it into the pan. This liquid will then become your gravy. You also get quite nice charred bar marks on the base of the pork.

5 The pork will take about 1 hour to cook. After 20 minutes, turn the temperature down to 220°C/gas 7. Once the pork is cooked, remove it from the oven on the rack and place on a piece of foil to save any juices. Allow to rest for at least 10 minutes.

6 To make the gravy, put the bones, liquid and vegetables from the roasting pan into a large frying pan or saucepan. Add some water to the roasting pan, as there will be some Marmite-like, sticky stuff on the bottom of the pan, which is very tasty. Bring to the boil on the hob, scraping all the goodness from the bottom of the roasting pan, then add this to the bones and vegetables.

7 Bring the gravy to the boil, shaking occasionally. Remove any oil or scum from the surface, then strain the contents, discarding all the vegetables and bones. You can reduce and then adjust the seasoning to taste.

honey-glazed roast barbary duck

Barbary ducks are not so fatty as ordinary ducks and have more flesh on the breast. Repeated brushing with a fragrant coating produces a wonderfully crisp skin with a deep, rich glaze. Allow several hours for the duck to dry; you can speed things up with a cool hair-dryer if necessary. This is delicious served with julienned leeks and carrots, and 'sweet potato mash' (see page 40).

Serves 3–4

Tools	Ingredients
colander	1 barbary duck, weighing 1.6–1.8kg.
paring knife	20–25 thin shreds orange peel, about 1cm long
pestle and mortar	150ml clear honey
ginger grater	4 tbsp rice wine or dry sherry
wire rack set over a shallow dish	4 tbsp white-wine vinegar
wide, flat brush	4 tbsp soy sauce
30 x 24cm roasting pan with rack	2 tsp fennel seeds, ground to a powder
lifting forks	4cm piece fresh ginger root, grated
carving knife	2 tsp sesame oil
poultry shears	200ml duck or chicken stock, preferably home-made
small saucepan	sea salt and freshly ground black pepper

1 Discard any lumps of fat from the duck's cavity. Put the duck in a colander and scald all over with boiling water. Pat dry thoroughly with a paper towel. Pierce the flesh evenly all over with the tip of a knife and insert the orange-peel shreds. Place the duck on a rack set over a dish.

2 Pour the honey into a small measuring jug. Stir in the rice wine or dry sherry, vinegar, soy sauce, fennel seeds, ginger root and sesame oil. Paint the mixture over the entire surface of the duck, including the crevices under the wings; reserve the remainder. Leave the duck on the rack in a cool, airy place to dry completely.

3 Preheat the oven to 220°C/gas 7. Brush the duck once more, using the liquid that has dripped into the dish.

4 Place the duck, breast-side up, on a rack in a roasting pan. Roast for 10 minutes, then turn the duck over, brush again with the coating mixture and roast for another 10 minutes.

5 Reduce the heat to 190°C/gas 5. Turn the duck breast-side up, brush, and roast for 30 minutes. Turn and roast for another 30 minutes, brushing every 10 minutes. Protect any blackened tips with foil.

6 Raise the heat to 200°C/gas 5 and turn the duck breast-side up. Brush again and roast for 10 minutes more. Carefully lift the duck onto a heated dish and leave to rest in a warm place for 10 minutes.

7 To carve the duck, remove the legs and the wings, leaving some of the breast meat attached to each wing. Remove the breast meat in two long pieces, then cut into bite-sized chunks, making sure a crispy piece of skin is attached to each chunk. Place all the duck pieces in a shallow serving dish and keep warm.

8 Pour any juices that have accumulated during carving into a small saucepan. Add the stock and the remaining coating. Simmer briskly until slightly reduced. Pour over the duck pieces and serve.

pots for braising and stewing

These pots form the backbone of any kitchen. They competently brown and simmer fragrant braises and stews, and come in all shapes and sizes, each with special characteristics. Materials are the same as those used for saucepans (see 'material choice', page 8), with the addition of ceramic. However, unlike saucepans these pots have small, ear-shaped handles, perhaps suggesting less input is required from the cook.

The ideal pot is one you can use on the hob or in the oven, and that is good looking enough to bring to the table. It is useful to have at least one pot that can be transferred from freezer to oven. You will need a couple of cooking pots, either in cast iron or stainless steel, for everyday use; a 6-litre pot serves 4–5 people, and a 3-litre pot serves 2–3 people. A shallow braising pan with a lid is also likely to earn its keep for big weekend breakfasts and for slow-cooked braises. A Dutch oven is a must for pot roasts and stews. Sizes range from a minuscule 2 litres to a vat-like 12 litres. Though it may seem unnecessarily large, the 8–9 litre size is well worth having – it can always double up as a soup, stock or even a pasta pot.

1 Braising pan This braiser can be used either on the hob or in the oven. The domed lid encourages condensation and maintains moist heat within the pot. Without the lid, the braiser can be used for frying. Made of 18/10 stainless steel, with a thick aluminium core extending up the sides of the pan, it conducts heat quickly and evenly.

2 Brittany pot Classic French dishes such as moules marinières, as well as stews and braises, are traditionally prepared in these rounded pots with gently flaring sides. Made of enamelled cast iron, this one comes in four colours.

1

2

3 Tagine A tagine is a uniquely shaped, thick earthenware pot, used in North Africa for the slow-cooked dish of the same name. The pot is traditionally used on an open fire. Very little liquid is needed as the conical lid provides a large cool surface on which steam condenses and then drips into the food below. The tall shape also keeps the lid cool at the top, so it can be lifted without a protective cloth.

Modified for use on the hob, this tagine has an enamelled cast-iron base that maintains even heat at low temperature; it can be used on any type of hob. The earthenware lid is glazed inside and out, making it durable and easy to clean.

3

4

4 Pot roaster This magificent 6-litre cooking pot is made of 18/10 stainless steel with an aluminium inner core for optimum heat conductivity. The core extends all the way up the sides of the pan (see 'material choice', stainless steel, page 8). The pot comes with an internal rack for easy removal of contents. It has ear-shaped, stay-cool handles and a well-fitting lid.

5 Non-stick casserole Made of titanium, the surface of this casserole is hard enough to withstand the use of metal tools. A rock-solid base browns and crisps at high temperatures but is equally good for gentle simmering. The glass lid, sold separately, is heat resistant up to 260°C so can be used in the oven. It is suitable for all hobs except the induction type.

5

Terminology

O **Braising** A moist cooking method in which food is placed in a covered dish with just enough liquid to produce steam during cooking.

O **Casserole** This is a somewhat confusing term that is used interchangeably with 'stew'. It refers to the cooking pot, the method of cooking and the finished dish itself.

O **Pot roasting** This is a similar technique to braising but relies more on moisture from the vegetables and meat being cooked than on added liquid.

O **Stewing** A slow, moist cooking method for tough meats and for developing rich flavours. Just enough liquid is added to cover the ingredients.

6 Enamelled Dutch oven Also known as a 'cocotte', this very heavy, enamelled cast-iron pot has tall, straight sides for holding substantial quantities of meat, vegetables and liquid. The heavy lid can either be sealed with a strip of dough or set slightly askew to allow steam to escape. A thick base allows for even heat transference on the hob. Use it for browning and slowly simmering stews.

6

7 Cast-iron Dutch oven This handsome pot in pre-seasoned, black cast iron was designed by Björn Dahlström and is destined to become a modern classic. Like the traditional Dutch oven, it has a thick, flat base for browning, and tall sides for holding a large volume of meat and liquid. The sides flare slightly to encourage evaporation. It is available in a 5-litre size only.

7

8 Brushed stainless-steel casserole Another modern classic by Björn Dahlström, this pot has the same minimalist lines as the cast-iron Dutch oven. Available in 5- and 8-litre sizes, it is made of superior 18/10 stainless steel with a thick aluminium core that extends all the way up the sides, giving good heat distribution throughout the pan.

8

9 Polished stainless-steel casserole Designed by Robert Welch, this gleaming pan combines looks with functionality. The base has a thick copper core for fast, even heat distribution, and the handles are set away from the pan for safety and comfort (use gloves after prolonged cooking). The lid is reversible for efficient storage and stacking. The casserole is available in 2.7-, 4.2- and 5.8-litre sizes.

9

clay pots

Together with iron, clay was one of the earliest materials used for making cooking pots, dating back to primitive times when food was cooked over an open fire or a bed of hot ashes. As their origin suggests, these homely pots are designed for simmering over a low gas flame or in the oven. Whatever their shape – tall, shallow, straight or bulbous – their virtue is that they absorb heat slowly and evenly, so food cooks uniformly without burning or drying out.

All clay pots are brittle, their strength depending on the temperature at which they were fired. The higher the temperature, the stronger the pot. The most brittle, and cheapest, are earthenware pots.

Glazed clay pots are non-porous, easier to clean and retain heat better than unglazed ones. Conversely, an unglazed surface absorbs heat more readily, so choose one with an unglazed base.

1 Bean pot/fait-tout This solid, spacious 4-litre pot truly lives up to its French name (fait tout meaning 'does all'). The bulging sides increase both the capacity and the actual heating surface, while the slightly narrower neck helps to slow evaporation. The bean pot is resistant to thermal shock so it can be transferred directly from the freezer to the oven. It is also dishwasher proof.

2 Marmite The tall, partially glazed marmite is traditionally used for hearty stews such as cassoulet or pot-au-feu. The lid is domed, which allows condensation to drip back into the pot and keep the contents moist. When the lid is removed, the large surface area created by the wide diameter and straight sides encourages evaporation and the formation of the authentic cassoulet crust.

3 Oval terrine An oval is a traditional shape for making and serving a rustic terrine or pâté of minced meat or fish. The tightly fitting lid rests on an inner lip and prevents food from drying out. Some terrines have a lid with a hole for steam to escape. The pot can also be used for stews. It is dishwasher proof, and can withstand temperatures from minus 20°C to 250°C.

4 Tontopf pot This unglazed pot is designed for making deliciously moist, oven-cooked stews with almost no water or fat. Before cooking, the entire pot is soaked in cold water, which is released as steam as the pot heats up. The steam condenses inside the lid and moisture drips onto the food.

5 Round terracotta pot Fired at 1050°C, this classic, straight-sided, glazed pot is resistant to fracturing and fluctuations of temperature. It is ideal for a winter meal for two, or for reheating small portions of leftover stew. It also makes an individual oven-to-table serving dish for hearty soups that need finishing off in the oven – onion soup, for example.

chicken tagine with preserved lemons

This wonderfully fragrant recipe was contributed by Claudia Roden, the acclaimed food writer who is credited with having 'single-handedly introduced the Western palate to Middle Eastern cuisine'. The word 'tagine' refers to both the stew and the pot in which it is cooked. The tagine pot (see page 102) gives the best results, but you can use a flameproof casserole into which the chicken fits snugly. If you use an earthenware tagine, there is a danger that it will crack if set over a gas flame. A heat diffuser will help prevent this; alternatively, do the preliminary cooking in a saucepan, then transfer the chicken to the earthenware pot and finish cooking in the oven.

Serves 4–6

Tools	Ingredients
grater	1 chicken, weighing about 1.8kg
garlic press	1 onion, grated or very finely chopped
pestle and mortar	2 garlic cloves, crushed
mezzaluna or cook's knife	1/4 tsp saffron pistils, crushed
tagine or 4.5-litre round or	1/2 tsp ground ginger
oval flameproof casserole	1 1/2 tsp ground cinnamon
2 large metal spoons	salt and freshly ground black pepper
cook's knife	good bunch coriander leaves, trimmed and finely chopped
	good bunch of flat-leaf parsley, trimmed and finely chopped
	peel of 1 1/2 preserved lemons (see below), cut into quarters
	75g green olives, soaked in 2 changes of water for 30 minutes, drained and rinsed

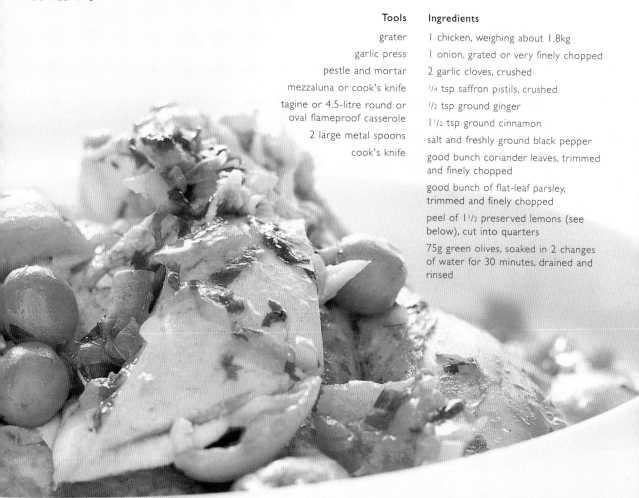

1 Put the chicken in a tagine or casserole with all the ingredients except the preserved lemons and olives. Half cover with water (about 300ml) and simmer on a medium to low heat, covered, for 1 hour, turning the chicken over a few times and adding more water if necessary.

2 Throw the lemon peel and olives into the sauce and continue to simmer for 20 minutes, or until the chicken is so tender the flesh pulls off the bone and the liquid is reduced.

3 Lift the chicken from the sauce and place in a shallow dish. Cut into serving-sized pieces and place in a serving dish or the base of a tagine. Using paper towels, blot any oil from the surface of the sauce. Pour the sauce over the chicken. Serve with couscous if you like.

Preserved lemons Wash and scrub four thick-skinned lemons. Cut into quarters lengthways but stop short at the stem end so the pieces are still attached. Stuff each lemon with 1 tablespoon of sea salt. Pack into a clean glass jar into which the lemons will just fit, pressing so they are squashed together. Seal the jar and leave for three or four days. They will start to release their juices and the skins will soften. Press them down as much as possible, and add enough fresh lemon juice to completely cover them. Seal the jar and leave in a cool place for at least a month. Rinse before using, to get rid of the salt.

beef pot roast with winter vegetables

Long, slow cooking in the moist environment of a covered pot produces meltingly tender meat from even the cheapest cuts. The meat is first browned and then gently cooked with vegetables and a relatively small amount of liquid. It bubbles away lazily, enriching the liquid in which it sits, and leaving you free to get on with other things. A sprinkling of finely chopped parsley, lemon zest and garlic added just before serving gives a lovely fresh flavour to the dish.

Serves 4

Tools	Ingredients
paring knife	1.6–1.8kg rolled beef, silverside or brisket
Dutch oven or casserole into which the meat fits snugly	4 fat garlic cloves, thinly sliced, plus 1 small garlic clove, finely chopped
tongs	about 20 rosemary leaves
cook's knife	2 tbsp vegetable oil
vegetable peeler	25g butter
citrus grater	1 red onion, finely chopped
mezzaluna	2 celery stalks, finely diced
conical sieve	2 carrots, finely diced
4 saucepans	small bunch of thyme
whisk	1 bay leaf
carving knife	2–3 strips thinly pared orange peel
	350ml red wine
	150ml meat stock, preferably home-made
	sea salt and freshly ground black pepper
	finely grated zest of 1 lemon
	3 tbsp chopped flat-leaf parsley
	1/2 tbsp plain flour
	To serve:
	16 baby carrots
	12 small potatoes, shaped into ovals
	1 Savoy cabbage, quartered and cut into ribbons
	knob of butter

1 Preheat the oven to 140°C/gas 1. Dry the meat thoroughly and make slits all over it with the tip of a small knife. Poke pieces of sliced garlic and the rosemary leaves into the slits, using the knife tip to embed them (a).

2 Heat the vegetable oil in a Dutch oven or heavy-based casserole. When it is very hot, add the meat and brown on all sides, turning with tongs (b). Transfer the meat to a plate.

3 Add half the butter to the pot. When it is sizzling, add the onion, celery and carrots and gently fry for about 5 minutes until soft.

4 Put the meat back in the pot, together with any juices that have accumulated. Add the thyme, bay leaf and orange peel, then pour in the wine and stock (c). The liquid should come no more than one-third of the way up the meat. Season with salt and freshly ground black pepper.

5 Bring the liquid to the boil, then cover with a tight-fitting lid and put in the oven. Cook for 3–3 1/2 hours, turning every 30 minutes or so.

6 Towards the end of the cooking time, mix together the lemon zest, parsley and chopped garlic. Mix the flour and remaining butter to a smooth paste. Cook the carrots, potatoes and cabbage until tender but still crisp and brightly coloured. Keep them warm in separate saucepans.

7 Remove the meat from the pot. Put it in a warm dish and leave to rest in a warm place for 10 minutes, loosely covered with foil.

8 Meanwhile, blot up any fat from the braising liquid with paper towels. Strain the vegetables into a saucepan, pressing them with the back of a spoon to extract all the liquid.

9 Bring the strained liquid to the boil, adding any juices that have flowed from the meat. Whisk in small pieces of the butter and flour paste, continuing to whisk until the sauce is smooth.

10 Carve the meat and arrange in overlapping slices on a warmed serving platter. Pour the sauce over the meat and sprinkle with the most of the parsley mixture.

11 Warm the vegetables through with butter, season with sea salt and freshly ground black pepper, and sprinkle with the remaining parsley.

baking and gratin dishes

These dishes are designed for baking food in the oven or browning toppings of bubbling cheese, crisp potato or crunchy breadcrumbs. Made of good-quality materials, such as porcelain or cast iron, gratin dishes conduct heat well and are not stressed by high temperatures. They are usually brought to the table so are made in attractive shapes and colours.

1 Rectangular ceramic gratin dishes These glazed dishes are strong enough to be transferred directly from freezer to oven. The rectangular shape makes efficient use of oven and fridge space, while gently sloping sides maximize the area for crusty topping and also allow stacking. A thick rim assists with lifting.

The large gratin dish is deep enough to take four or five layers of lasagne. The slightly rounded interior makes serving and cleaning easier.

2 Oval ceramic gratin dishes These are the classic shape for a gratin and are versatile enough to be used as serving dishes or even for carving a small roast. The dishes can be transferred directly from freezer to oven. They conduct heat evenly and retain it well, ensuring food remains warm at the table.

3 Porcelain soufflé dishes Round, deep, and straight sided, these dishes expose soufflé mixtures to maximum heat. This coagulates the egg proteins before the air incorporated during whisking has time to escape. The smooth porcelain interior allows the expanding mixture to rise up the dish. It is available in several sizes, but the preferred one is 0.9 litre. Anything larger and you risk the inside not being properly cooked.

4 Enamelled cast-iron egg dish This shallow dish is specially designed for cooking eggs, either in the oven or on the hob. Widely flaring sides make serving and cleaning easier, but more importantly they increase the surface area and expose the eggs to maximum heat so they cook evenly.

5 Enamelled cast-iron baking dish The deep sides of this dish make it particularly useful for baking eggs that have a layer of vegetables, such as spinach, underneath, or for individual portions of lasagne.

6 Porcelain ramekins These smooth, straight-sided ramekins are used for individual soufflés, as well as baked custards or crème brûlées. Egg-based dishes such as these are cooked in a roasting pan filled with enough hot water to come halfway up the sides of the ramekins. The ramekins have a slightly roughened base to prevent a vacuum forming and making it difficult to lift them from the water bath.

7 Porcelain oval gratin dishes Available in several sizes, these classic white gratin dishes have a beautiful shape. The fluted handles merge with the sides of the dish, which slope gracefully outwards to increase the surface area for browning. The sloping sides increase the surface area.

8 Porcelain chocolate pots These elegant pots are traditionally used for rich chocolate desserts, as well as baked creams and custards.

Gratin dishes are shallow so they fit under the grill or close to the top of the oven. Handles are small and project outwards rather than upwards so food can be positioned close to the grill. Some dishes have a rim round the top edge to make them easy to grasp while wearing an oven glove.

The most indispensable dishes to have are a set of small, medium and large ceramic gratin dishes, either rectangular or square. They will earn their keep by doubling up as serving dishes for vegetables, rice and salads. A set of six or eight individual-sized ramekins is also useful, not only for sweet or savoury baked dishes, but also for serving small snacks to go with drinks.

9 Earthenware potato baker
Known in France as a 'diable', this porous, unglazed earthenware baker seals in moisture and effectively steam-cooks the contents. By doing so it conserves both flavour and aroma. To work well, the size and shape of the baker should closely follow those of the contents. There are different shaped bakers for cooking chicken and fish.

10 Glazed earthenware basins
These are the classic basins for traditional steamed puddings. The mixture is covered with pleated greaseproof paper, held in place with string tied under the thick rim, which is designed for the purpose. These basins are also ideal for chilled summer pudding, and can double as mixing bowls.

11 Cast-iron rectangular terrine
This dish is designed for baking and shaping the dense mixture of finely chopped vegetables, meat or fish that constitutes a terrine. Cast iron permits the necessary slow, even cooking, while the elongated shape facilitates slicing the terrine into neat, cracker-sized portions.

12 Non-stick steel meat loaf pan
This two-part pan has a ridged, perforated base for draining away the fatty liquid that is the bane of cooking a meat loaf. The outer pan doubles as a bread pan.

13 Aluminium pudding basins
These basins can be used for old-fashioned steamed puddings, and as cold moulds for chilled custards and mousses. Aluminium is not a suitable material for cooking fruit puddings unless lined with greaseproof paper (see 'material choice', page 8).

fresh shell bean gratin

Alice Waters is one of America's favourite chefs. Described as 'poetic', 'visionary' and 'passionate', her cooking is based on the belief that optimal flavour and environmental harmony go hand in hand. This comforting supper dish is typical of her cooking. You will need a gratin dish about 5cm deep and 23cm square. Fresh shell beans are available in late summer and early autumn. Use a mixture of beans of varying colours. You will need 900g–1.3kg in their pods, which should provide 450–500g when shelled. You can also make the gratin with dried beans. Soak 225g beans (separately, if using a mixture) overnight. Drain and boil rapidly in fresh water for 20 minutes. Drain again and begin cooking with step 1.

Serves 4–6

Tools

medium-sized saucepans for each type of bean
strainer
jug or bowl
cook's knife
paring knife
medium frying pan
wooden spoon
1.5 litre gratin dish

Ingredients

450–500g podded fresh shell beans, such as cannellini, flageolet and borlotti

salt

6 tbsp olive oil

1/2 onion, finely chopped

4 garlic cloves, cut into slivers

1–2 sage leaves, chopped

125–150g greens such as chard, broccoli raab, mustard greens, turnip tops, sliced into ribbons (optional)

2 tomatoes, roughly chopped

8 tbsp toasted breadcrumbs (see below)

1 Put the beans in a saucepan with just enough water to cover by 2.5cm (fresh shell beans absorb very little water). When they have come to the boil, add salt and 2 tablespoons of the olive oil, and lower the heat to a simmer. Cook until the beans are tender, about 30 minutes. Drain the beans in a strainer set over a measuring jug, and save their liquid.

2 Preheat the oven to 180°C/gas 4. While the beans are cooking, gently fry the onion in 2 tablespoons of olive oil, with the garlic, sage leaves and some salt, until the onion is soft and translucent. If you wish, cook a small bunch of greens with the onion; add a little of the bean water along with them if you do.

3 When the onion is cooked, add the tomatoes, raise the heat, and cook for a minute or two more.

4 Combine the beans in a gratin dish with the onions, tomatoes and greens, if using. Add enough bean water to almost cover. Taste, correct the seasoning, and pour the rest of the olive oil over the gratin.

5 Cover the top with toasted breadcrumbs and bake for 45 minutes. Check occasionally and moisten with more bean water if the gratin seems to be drying out too much.

Toasted breadcrumbs Preheat the oven to 150°C. Remove the crust from stale levain bread or other country-style bread. Shred into small pieces and either chop it by hand or in a food processor, or leave in rough chunks depending on use. Toss with a pinch of salt and a little olive oil to coat the bread. Spread the crumbs on a baking sheet in a thin layer. Bake until golden brown, tossing every 10 minutes.

dough making

tools for pizza and pasta

There is no mystique to making the doughs for these all-time comforters – just chemistry, patience and a sense of touch. The most important piece of equipment is your hands. Other tools just help things along.

For success with home-made pizza dough, bake your pizza on a baking stone preheated in an oven set at the highest temperature possible. With luck, the result will match the deliciously crisp crust produced by the intense heat of a wood-fired brick oven.

Making your own pasta dough takes time but is a particularly relaxing and satisfying experience. The result will be far superior to the so-called 'fresh' pasta sold by supermarkets.

1 Perforated pizza pan The holes in this pan allow heat and air to reach the centre of the dough, resulting in a crisper crust than is possible with a solid baking sheet. The pan is particularly good for large pizzas.

2 Pizza stone Preheated in a very hot oven, this thick, unglazed ceramic slab draws moisture from the dough, producing a crisp yet chewy crust. It is available in diameters of 32–40cm.

3 Pizza peel/paddle This flat tool has a chamfered edge that slides smoothly under a pizza as you lift it from the stone. Peels are also made of wood, which remains cooler in use.

4 Ravioli tray Made of cast aluminium, this 36-square tray produces ravioli of a uniform size and shape. The wide, flat edges between the indentations increase the area of contact between the layers of dough and reduce the risk of leaks.

5 Pasta machine This hand-cranked pasta machine speeds the process of rolling and cutting dough. The machine has graduated openings that are used successively to reduce the dough to the desired thickness. Attachable cutters slice it into ribbons of different widths.

6 Wooden rollers These pleasing wooden rollers are deeply etched for hand-cutting dough into ribbons of various widths. The cutting edges are quite fragile and may chip if not handled with care.

7 Pasta cutting wheels This superb hand-crafted tool has two detachable brass wheels – one plain and one zigzagged for cutting saw-edged ribbons or ravioli. Unlike mass-produced cutters, the wheels have well-defined edges that produce a very clean cut. Being thick and heavy, brass remains cooler in use than lighter metals. This also contributes to a clean cut.

8 Ravioli cutter If you like extra-large pillows of ravioli, this 6.5cm-square cutter, made of cast aluminium, is the tool to use.

fresh pasta

Making fresh pasta is really no more of a challenge than making pastry, especially if you use a machine to help you thin and cut the dough. The secret is in the kneading and gradual thinning. You must close the rollers a notch at a time, resisting any temptation to skip a notch.

Pasta responds to warmth so never work it on a marble or metal surface. Use a large wooden board or other smooth, relatively warm material. You need plenty of space for laying out the strips of pasta, and plenty of clean, dry tea towels on which to lay them.

For the best results use Italian '00' flour, allowing 100g for each large egg. That said, it is almost impossible to predict exactly how much flour will be needed. You need enough to produce a dough that is neither too dry nor too sticky. Start off with a little less flour – you can always add more. If you add it all at once and the dough is too dry, you will have to start again.

Makes enough for 4 to 6 servings

Tools	Ingredients
large wooden board	300g Italian '00' flour
dough scraper	3 large eggs, at room
hand-cranked pasta machine	temperature

1 Pour the flour onto a wooden surface, shaping it into a mound with a central well. Break the eggs into the well and beat lightly with a fork. When evenly mixed, start drawing some of the flour over the eggs (a). Continue until the eggs are no longer runny.

2 Quickly draw the sides of the mound over the eggs, leaving a little flour on the side to use if the dough is too sticky. Work the eggs and flour together until smoothly integrated, adding the reserved flour if necessary (b). Wrap the dough in clingfilm and scrape the surface clean.

3 Knead the dough by pushing forward against it with the heel of your hand, then fold it in half, give it a half turn and push forward again (c). Repeat, turning in the same direction, for 15 minutes or until the dough is silky smooth and elastic.

4 Cut the dough into at least six pieces. Flatten one and wrap the rest separately in clingfilm. Fold the flat piece in three (d) and pass it lengthways through the pasta machine, set at the widest opening (e). Repeat three or four times, folding the dough in thirds each time. Put the strips on a tea towel and repeat with the other pieces of dough.

5 Close the rollers by one notch and run all the strips through again, this time without folding them. Close the opening by another notch and repeat the procedure. Continue until the rollers are at the narrowest setting.

6 To make ribbons, cut the pasta into 30cm strips and feed through the cutter of your choice (f). As the ribbons emerge, separate them carefully and spread out on tea towels.

7 To dry the pasta, coil a few ribbons into a nest and leave to dry for 24 hours, making sure the nests do not touch. Store in an airtight container.

ricotta and mint tortelloni

Marcella Hazan is the doyenne of Italian cookery and one of the world's most respected food writers. In her delectable home-made tortelloni, silky, golden egg pasta is stuffed with ricotta cheese, mint, onion and garlic. A bay leaf-scented tomato sauce provides the perfect complement. As Marcella says, 'This has the briskest, lightest flavour of any stuffed pasta I know'. The sauce can be cooked one or two days in advance, and reheated at a gentle simmer before tossing with the pasta. The tortelloni can be made as far ahead as early in the morning, if you are serving them for dinner.

Makes about 36 tortelloni to serve 6 as an appetizer or 4 as a main course

Note Pasta that is going to be stuffed should be soft and sticky, so the procedure given on page 113 must be adjusted as follows: take one piece of dough at a time through the entire thinning process and, before going on to the next piece, cut it and stuff it as described below.

1 Wrap the ricotta tightly in a layer of cheesecloth and drain for 30 minutes, as in the recipe for 'yogurt cheese' on page 58. Place the ricotta in a bowl, add the nutmeg, mint, egg yolk, salt and pepper, and mix well.

2 Put the butter and onion in a small frying pan, turn the heat to medium, and cook the onion, stirring occasionally, until it turns a pale gold. Add the garlic and cook it, stirring frequently, until it is a shade of gold paler than the onion. Empty the contents of the pan into the ricotta mixture, stirring with a wooden spoon until uniformly mixed.

3 Following the instructions on page 113, make the dough with the eggs, flour and the extra milk, then mix and knead it. Cut the dough into four pieces and take one piece through the entire rolling, folding and thinning process, taking it down to the thinnest notch setting. Keep the rest of the dough covered in cling film.

4 Lay a 15cm-wide, long strip of dough on a clean tea towel. Dot with a row of cherry-sized pellets of stuffing, setting them down 6cm apart and 3cm from one long edge of the rectangle (a).

5 When you have distributed as many dots of stuffing that will fit along the strip, bring the edge furthest from the stuffing over them and join it to the other edge (b). Force the air from between the bulges of stuffing with the edge of your hand and press the edges together gently but firmly. Run a fluted pastry wheel down the edge to trim and seal it, then run the wheel crossways, midway between each bulge of stuffing (c). Press the edges with your fingertip, then spread the tortelloni out on tea towels, making sure they do not touch.

6 Now repeat the entire thinning, stuffing and cutting process with the remaining pieces of dough. The tortelloni can be cooked immediately or after several hours. If you are going to cook them later, turn them over every 15 minutes or so.

7 To make the sauce, put the 25g of butter and 1 1/2 tablespoons of oil in a medium frying pan over medium-high heat. Cook the onion, stirring, until it turns a medium gold. Add the bay leaves and cook for a few seconds, turning, then add the tomatoes, salt and pepper. Cook at a steady but gentle simmer, stirring periodically, for about 15–20 minutes, until the fat floats free of the tomatoes.

8 Cook the tortelloni in a large saucepan of boiling, salted water, adding 1 tablespoon of olive oil. If you are cooking them some hours after making them, they will take a little longer than when very fresh. Taste one after about 3 minutes, and if necessary continue cooking until they are tender, but retain some firmness to the bite. Retrieve them from the saucepan with a perforated spoon or wire strainer, gently transferring them to a colander (d).

9 As soon as the tortelloni are done, place in a warm serving platter, and gently toss with 15g of butter, the tomato sauce and grated Parmigiano-Reggiano. Serve at once.

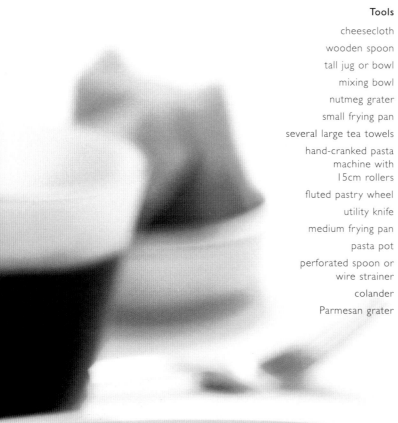

Tools	Ingredients
cheesecloth	*For the stuffing:*
wooden spoon	225g wholemilk ricotta
tall jug or bowl	1/8 tsp freshly grated nutmeg
mixing bowl	4 tsp chopped fresh mint leaves
nutmeg grater	1 egg yolk
small frying pan	salt and freshly ground black pepper
several large tea towels	15g butter
hand-cranked pasta machine with 15cm rollers	2 tbsp finely chopped onion
	1/2 tsp chopped garlic
fluted pastry wheel	*For the wrappers:*
utility knife	150–200g Italian '00' flour
medium frying pan	2 large eggs at room temperature
pasta pot	1 tbsp milk
perforated spoon or wire strainer	*For cooking and saucing the pasta:*
	25g butter for the sauce, 15g for tossing
colander	1 1/2 tbsp extra-virgin olive oil for the sauce, 1 tbsp for the pasta
Parmesan grater	1/2 small onion, finely chopped
	4 bay leaves
	350g large, firm, ripe tomatoes, skinned, deseeded and chopped
	salt and freshly ground black pepper
	50g freshly grated Parmigiano-Reggiano

The smell and texture of fresh yeast, the rhythmic kneading, the perfect curve of risen dough and the transformation to a fine-tasting, crusty loaf make breadmaking the most sensuous of culinary pleasures.

bread tins

Although bread dough is dense enough to retain its shape when baked on a flat sheet, you can control its shape more precisely, and even the density of crumb, by using a tin. An open rectangular tin confines the base and sides of a loaf, while allowing the top to expand upwards and develop a crust. An enclosed tin limits the amount of expansion and produces a loaf with a denser crumb.

If you are new to bread making, start off with two or three rectangular, medium-sized tins – after all, if you are making one loaf, you might as well make two or three. As you progress, you may want to add a larger tin, and possibly tins for baguettes or brioches.

Rectangular tins should have firmly welded seams and a reinforced, rolled rim. A dimpled surface helps prevent sticking. A non-stick lining also helps in this respect, but is unlikely to be foolproof, and will eventually wear out. Brushing or spraying non-stick tins with oil is always a good idea.

If you bake bread regularly it is worth buying professional, heavy-grade tins. They will not warp or twist, and in time will develop a smooth patina of their own, so you won't need to grease them.

Bread tins come in a range of sizes; make sure you choose the right size for the loaf you intend to cook. The tin should be just over half full when the knocked-back dough is placed in it.

1 Brioche tin This tin has flared, fluted sides and is used for baking brioche, a soft dough enriched with butter and eggs. The sides are taller than the width of the base, which permits maximum rising and exposes a large area of dough to the heat, so the edges set quickly. Tins come in seven sizes, from 7.5 to 20cm in diameter.

2 Non-stick bread tins Solidly made, these rectangular tins have corners reinforced by their own pleats, sturdy rolled rims and two layers of non-stick coating. They are available in two sizes: 17 x 11 x 8cm and 19 x 12 x 9cm.

3 Non-stick French bread tin This 40cm, finely perforated tin is designed to hold two medium-length baguettes. If you choose a longer tin, make sure it will fit into your oven.

4 Hinged tin Take out the end pins of this tinned-steel tin and the sides fall away, allowing you to remove the loaf easily. It measures 30 x 11 x 7.5cm, and can also be used for terrines and cakes.

Bread-tin materials Blued or blackened steel has been heated to a very high temperature, which creates an ultra-smooth oxidized surface that has some resistance to rust. It is an excellent conductor of heat. Tinned steel has a coating of tin, as the name suggests. Before use, bread tins made of tinned steel need to be washed and dried carefully. Aluminium is a lightweight material and an excellent conductor of heat, but it lacks strength on its own. To compensate, manufacturers sometimes use aluminium to coat bread tins made of steel plate.

cake tins and trays

Cake baking is a precise skill requiring accuracy of weighing, temperature and tin size. Tins of the same volume can have different dimensions – one may be wide and shallow, another narrow and deep. A mixture intended to cook quickly in a shallow tin will not cook properly in a tin that is too deep, and vice versa. A good recipe will specify the dimensions of the tin, not just the volume.

The most useful tins to have are a pair of round, shallow, 20cm tins for sponge cakes, a deep, 23 or 25cm tin for fruit cake, a Swiss roll tin and perhaps a 23cm springform tin for easy release of moulded cakes and desserts. One or two 12-cup trays are useful for muffins, small cakes and tarts, or dough left over from a large cake. Tins with a non-stick surface may not be foolproof, but are worth having nevertheless. For choice of materials, see 'Bread-tin materials', page 117.

1 Joined small tins These differently shaped individual tins are joined together in a row for convenience. Choose from boats, rectangles, waisted ovals and many more. Once you have one sort, you'll want to collect more.

2 Foil and paper cups Useful for light mixes that cook very quickly, these can be placed on a baking sheet or in the indented cups of a muffin tray. If they are left in place until ready to eat, paper cups prevent the cakes from drying out. Children love peeling them off.

3 English bun tray This 12-cup, non-stick tray is ideal for small cakes, tarts and mini-quiches. The ridged handles make the tray easier to grip when sliding it in and out of the oven.

4 Yorkshire pudding tray Similar to the English bun tray, this one has four shallow, flat-bottomed cups for making single portions of Yorkshire pudding. The tray can also be used for baking small sponge cakes, tarts and quiches.

5 Cooling racks An elevated wire rack speeds cooling of cakes by allowing steam to evaporate from all surfaces. A very fragile cake may be damaged by the wires, so cover the rack with a layer of greaseproof paper before placing the cake on it. The paper will absorb evaporating steam.

6 Popover/muffin tray Air circulates quickly between these individual cups pressed into a heavy, cast-iron sheet, promoting rapid rising and setting of dough. The flared, 4cm deep sides increase surface area, which encourages dough to rise and moisture to evaporate.

Swedish dill bread

Successful food writers in their own right, Eric Treuille and Ursula Ferrigno have collaborated on a best-selling breadmaking book and they both teach baking – Ursula in her native Italy and Eric at the popular Books for Cooks Cookery School in London. Their recipe for Swedish dill bread is, quite simply, superb. Enriched with cream cheese, butter and eggs, and subtly scented with dill, this bread has a moist crumb, light texture and a golden crust studded with toasted onion. It makes a wonderful accompaniment to smoked salmon. A lightly greased non-stick loaf tin guarantees a cleanly turned out loaf.

Makes 1 loaf

Tools	Ingredients
small and large bowls	2 tsp dried yeast
sieve	100ml tepid water
wooden spoon	500g strong white flour
flour dredger	1 tsp salt
brush for greasing	2 tbsp chopped fresh dill
19 x 12 x 9cm non-stick loaf tin	150g cream cheese, at room temperature
	2 onions, roughly chopped
wire rack	25g unsalted butter, at room temperature, plus extra for greasing tin
	1 egg, beaten

1 Sprinkle the yeast into the water in a small bowl. Leave for 5 minutes, then stir until dissolved.

2 Sift the flour and salt together in a large bowl. Make a well in the centre and add the dill, cream cheese, onions, butter, egg and yeasted water. Use a wooden spoon to mix all the ingredients together with the flour to form a stiff, sticky dough.

3 Turn the dough onto a lightly floured work surface. Gather into a ball and then flatten. Shape the dough by folding one half over the other, bringing the top towards you.

4 Use the heel of your working hand to push the dough away from you (a). At the same time, use the other hand to rotate the dough slightly towards you, guiding it slowly round in a circle. Repeat the folding, pushing and rotating for at least 10 minutes until the dough is silky smooth.

5 Put the dough in a clean bowl and cover with a tea towel. Leave the dough to rise until it has doubled in size, about 1 1/2 hours.

6 Grease a loaf tin with butter. Knock back the dough, then leave to rest for 10 minutes.

7 With the lightly floured palm of your hand, flatten the dough to expel any gas bubbles (b). Keep it in a round shape by exerting even pressure. Fold one edge of the dough to the centre. Press gently to seal the fold.

8 Fold the other half of the dough inwards so the two folds overlap along the middle of the loaf (c). Gently press along the length of the outer seam to seal the two folds together.

9 Place the dough seam-side down on the work surface. Shape to an even thickness. Lift the dough, tuck under the ends and place it in the prepared tin, seam-side down (d). Cover with a tea towel. Leave to prove until the dough has risen 1cm above the top of the tin, about 1 1/2 hours.

10 Preheat the oven to 180°C/gas 4. Bake the loaf for 45 minutes to 1 hour until deeply golden and hollow-sounding when tapped underneath. Turn out on a wire rack and leave to cool.

7 Angel food cake tin The tube allows heat to penetrate to the centre of the cake and provides another surface for the mixture to cling to as it rises. The tube projects beyond the rim so when the tin is inverted to cool the cake, air can pass beneath it. Some tins have small feet on the rim for better balance when inverted.

8 Deep, round cake tins Dense fruit-cake mixtures need long cooking, so should be baked in a deep, heavy-gauge tin to prevent scorching. These tins have a removable base and a reinforced, rolled rim that helps to maintain their shape.

9 Springform tin This is invaluable for fragile cakes that are hard to unmould. When the clip is unbuckled, the sides of the tin move out from the base, leaving behind a perfectly formed cake. Made of heavy-gauge steel with a durable non-stick coating inside and out, this heavy-duty tin comes with an additional tube base embossed with swirling flutes. It is ideal for cheesecake or mousse-like cakes.

10 Swiss roll tin Extremely shallow, this rectangular tin is specially designed for cooking the thin layer of sponge needed for a Swiss roll. It is made from heavy-gauge tinned steel, which conducts heat quickly and evenly, and will not warp or twist.

11 Shallow cake tin This is used for quickly cooked mixtures such as sponge cakes and sponge sandwiches. It is best to buy a pair. Although it has a non-stick surface, it still needs greasing.

12 Madeleine tray The scallop-shaped, fluted indentations increase the area that is exposed to heat. This allows the batter to rise quickly in the middle and produce the characteristic madeleine shapes.

tart tins and pie plates

For a meltingly crisp, golden-brown pastry case, use a fluted metal tin with a removable base. Some cooks use a bottomless metal ring set directly on a baking sheet. Though they are attractive, tart dishes made of fluted porcelain absorb heat more slowly than metal and do not produce such a crisp crust.

The most useful diameters for tart tins are 23 and 25cm. If you ever need to cater for a crowd, you might also want to consider a 30cm tin. A high-sided tart tin comes in handy for making quiches. If you are partial to pies, deep and shallow ceramic pie dishes are worth buying, as is a metal pie plate for that spur-of-the-moment pie.

Rigid metal baking trays or sheets are essential for baking small pastry shapes, biscuits and hand-formed breads. They also provide porcelain dishes with a boost of heat from below, which helps to cook the base. It's worth buying two baking trays so you can load one while the other is in the oven. Never put two in the oven simultaneously – the top one will prevent heat circulating over the lower, and you'll end up with unevenly cooked food. Buy the largest baking tray your oven will accommodate, but allow at least 5cm all round for air circulation.

1 Deep fluted tart tins The fluted sides of these metal tins almost double the surface area exposed to heat. This encourages the crust to set more quickly. Being deep, the sides make a particularly strong crust, which is useful for cream- or egg-based fillings containing solid pieces of food. The bases of these tins are removable (see 2).

2 Shallow fluted tart tins Perfect for glazed fruit tarts or shallow custard-filled tarts, these tins are available in sizes ranging from 11 to 31cm. As with the deep-fluted tins, the bases are removable for easy unmoulding. Stand the tin on a jam jar and ease the outer ring down. You can leave the tart on the base when you transfer it to a serving plate.

3 Non-stick sponge tart tin This warp-free tin with a raised centre is used for baking those slightly old-fashioned whisked sponge cases that you load up with whipped cream and fruit. Once turned out, the base is left upside down, leaving a raised rim surrounding a circle for the filling. The base has a dimpled surface, which makes unmoulding easier.

4 Tarte tatin tin Made of copper lined with stainless steel, this elegant pan is ideal for baking the upside-down apple cake known as 'tarte tatin', because copper quickly conducts the high heat necessary for caramelizing syrupy juices. A wide base and shallow sides provide a large surface area, which allows the tart to cook evenly through to the centre.

5 Deep pie dish This is one of those impeccably designed dishes that get handed down from generation to generation. It is made of thick, glazed ceramic, which allows steady heat to penetrate the centre of the pie without burning the crust. The wide, flat rim supports the top layer of pastry and gives a generous seal, while the gently rounded interior makes serving and cleaning easier.

6 Pie bird The purpose of this porcelain bird is to support the top crust and vent the steam that would otherwise make the crust soggy. The slightly arced base allows steam to travel upwards and out through the beak. Make sure the beak is wide open. You can also buy special funnels that serve the same purpose.

7 Shallow pie dish Like the deep dish (5), this classic piece of bakeware is made of thick, glazed ceramic with a flat rim for sealing double-crust pies. The round, shallow shape makes it a versatile dish – it can double up as a gratin dish and is elegant enough to be used as a serving bowl for vegetables, salad or fruit.

8 Pie plates These lovely traditional tinned-steel plates are for baking shallow, double-crust pies or open tarts – the kind your grandmother used to make. They are available in a range of sizes, from a single serving to a family-sized 30cm.

9 Non-stick pie plate with insert This pie plate is supplied with a useful perforated insert that can be used on its own instead of baking 'beans' (see page 126) when baking an unfilled pastry case.

10 Baking sheets These heavy-duty baking sheets absorb and transmit the heat necessary for setting, crisping and browning doughs of various kinds. The upper sheet is made of tinned steel and the lower of blackened steel (see 'bread tins', page 117). They are rigid enough not to warp or twist, and have a slightly inclined edge that makes them easier to grip. Biscuit or baking trays perform a similar function, but they have a shallow, fully turned-up edge to prevent runny doughs from overflowing and cooked biscuits from sliding off the tray.

a

b

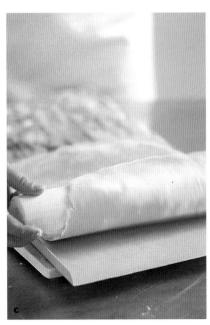

c

leek and peppercorn tart

A mouthwatering supper-time treat, this tart is made with rich shortcrust pastry. For maximum crispness, the pastry is rolled as thinly as possible and baked directly on a baking sheet at a high temperature. The leeks must be small and thinly sliced so they cook through. They will be tender but still crisp. The smoky flavour of green peppercorns is delicious with leeks and cheese.

Serves 4–6 as a light meal

Tools	Ingredients
flour sifter or sieve	225g plain unbleached flour
mixing bowl	1/4 tsp each salt and sugar
pastry blender	150g butter
coarse grater	3 tbsp iced water
pestle and mortar	100g Cheddar cheese
cook's knife	100g mozzarella cheese
utility knife	1 1/2 tsp dried green peppercorns
flour dredger	salt
rolling pin	3 small leeks, weighing about 250g
baking sheet	in total
small flat whisk	50g pancetta
pastry brush	salt
	2 tsp fresh thyme leaves
	beaten egg yolk, to glaze

1 Sift the flour, salt and sugar into a bowl. Using a pastry blender if you wish, work in half the butter until the mixture resembles coarse crumbs (a). Briefly work in the remaining butter, leaving it slightly unevenly mixed. Lightly stir in the water to form a soft dough. Wrap in cling film and chill for 1 hour.

2 Grate the cheeses, using the coarse blade of a grater. Crush the peppercorns with a pestle and mortar. Trim the leeks and slice in half lengthways, then crossways into 2cm slices. You will need 175g of prepared leek. Cut the pancetta into bite-sized pieces.

3 Preheat the oven to 240°C/gas 9. Roll out the dough on a floured surface as thinly as possible to form a 31cm square (b). Carefully drape the dough over a rolling pin and place on a baking sheet (c). Trim the edges neatly.

4 Leaving a 1.5cm border all round, scatter the cheeses evenly over the dough. Sprinkle with the peppercorns and a little salt to taste, then add the leeks, spreading them out evenly. Sprinkle with the pancetta and thyme.

5 Fold up the edges of the pastry to slightly enclose the filling, folding the corners to a pleat. Brush the edges with the egg yolk.

6 Bake for 20 minutes until the pastry is golden and the leeks look slightly charred. Serve hot or warm.

pastry paraphernalia

Making pastry is a multi-stage process. You will need tools for blending, rolling, cutting, crimping, brushing and scraping. Though much of this work can be done with your hands, using these tools makes life easier and gives a neater result.

A rolling pin is a must. Pastry can be rolled with a broom handle or milk bottle, but neither are the ideal texture, length or diameter. Rolling pins should be smooth to the touch, and longer than the area covered by the dough once it is rolled out. Metal rolling pins are cooler than wooden ones, but because wood is a poor conductor of heat, a wooden pin is pretty cool too. The pin should be heavy enough to do its job without needing undue pressure from you. Though they can make pins more comfortable to use, handles reduce the width of the rolling surface or result in an unnecessarily long pin, which may be difficult to store.

1 Dough scraper Originally used for measuring and dividing dough into equal pieces, this traditional tool is now more often used as a scraper, though it still comes in handy for checking your dough is the right size.

2 Pastry wheel A fluted wheel gives a zigzag edge to lattice strips, pasta ribbons and ravioli squares. The safety guard prevents your finger slipping onto the wheel.

3 Lattice cutter This ingenious tool saves the work of hand-weaving a lattice topping for a tart. Toothed wheels produce a series of broken lines as you roll the cutter over the dough. Gently lift and stretch the dough to open out the lattice.

4 Flexible palette knife Use this tool for evenly spreading and smoothing the surface of soft mixtures and toppings. Wetting the blade helps prevent sticking.

5 Pastry blender A blender is useful for working fat into flour if your fingertips aren't up to it.

6 Natural bristle pastry brushes Bristles reach into crevices and coat surfaces evenly. These brushes are indispensable for anointing pastry, dusting flour or greasing tins. Wash and dry them carefully after use.

Pastry cutters
7 This covetable professional set includes cutters of every conceivable size. Use them to cut circles not only from dough, but also from firm fleshed vegetables, pineapple, aspic and hard-boiled eggs. A rolled top edge maintains their shape.
8 More homely is this set of three crinkle cutters. Make sure you wash and dry them carefully after use to avoid rusting.
9 This double-ringed doughnut cutter prevents the off-centre holes that may occur when using two separate cutters.

11 Wooden rolling pin This 38cm professional pin sacrifices no rolling surface to handles.

10 Marble pastry board Cool, smooth marble is the ideal surface on which to roll pastry. It needs very little flouring to prevent sticking.

12 Aluminium baking 'beans' These small metal weights help to prevent blistering and shrinking in the first stage of baking a pastry case. Spread them thickly over the base of a foil-lined case, packing them against the sides, and remove them with the foil once the pastry has set.

moulding
and
shaping

taking shape

Moulded foods such as mousses, custards and jellies seem to hark back to a more leisurely era when there was time for the setting and chilling these dishes need. Whether sweet or savoury, such foods are by their very nature soft and delicate, and perhaps have been somewhat ousted from modern cooking with its insistence on speedy chargrilling and stir-frying, and bold, assertive flavours.

Despite changing trends, moulds do have a place in today's kitchens, even if for only a simple concoction such as a child's birthday jelly. And let's not forget the most basic of modern moulds – the ice-cube tray. Moulds may either be decorative or utilitarian, tall or shallow, patterned or plain. They are often made of metals such as aluminium or copper, because these react very quickly to heat or cold; porcelain or glass is used where heat or cold needs to be retained. Confectionery moulds are made of tinned steel, plastic or rubber. Moulds are often made in the shape of a fish or fruit to indicate the nature of the dish.

Mixtures for tall or ornate moulds need to be more firmly set than for shallow ones, as they are more likely to collapse or leave part of their contents trapped in an intricate crevice. The smoother and shallower the mould, the easier it is to turn out.

I Giant ice-cube tray This brilliant ice-cube tray is flexible so you can remove cubes individually, and is supplied with a metal tray so it stays flat in the freezer.

2 Fish mould Ornate and versatile, this mould is equally suitable for a grown-up fish mousse or a bright orange childrens' jelly.

3 Ring moulds These seamless aluminium moulds are designed for baking savarins and babas – rich, yeasted cakes that are drenched in syrup or rum after cooking. The cake remains upside down after turning out and the depression in the centre is piled high with whipped cream and/or fruit. A wide, shallow trough and a thick central tube allow maximum exposure to heat, so the mixture cooks quickly as it rises. Ring moulds can also be used for mousses, custards or rice.

4 Bombe mould This smooth, spherical mould with a rounded top has a tightly fitting lid to prevent ice crystals forming during storage.

5 Charlotte mould To make a charlotte, this bucket-shaped aluminium mould is lined with buttered bread or sponge fingers and then filled with a fruit purée or mousse. The outwardly sloping sides make it easier to line and also allow it to be lifted free of its contents once inverted. Charlottes may be served uncooked and chilled, or baked in the oven and served hot – hence the mould's two heart-shaped handles. Either way, aluminium is an excellent conductor, speeding the penetration of heat or cold as appropriate.

6 Dariole moulds
These small, simple aluminium moulds are good conductors of heat or cold. Use them for making tiny rum babas (but fill only halfway and allow the dough to rise before baking), small sponge puddings, timbales, jellies and crème caramels.

7 Heart mould
A tool for romantic cooks, this mould is ideal for sweet or savoury dishes to celebrate Valentine's Day or anniversaries.

8 Jelly/blancmange moulds
These aluminium moulds are embossed with simple but decorative patterns well suited to a jelly or blancmange. Make sure the top of the unfilled mould is level so that when inverted it does not wobble while the contents are setting.

presses and extruders

Some foods depend on special shaping – piped cake icing, for example. Other foods, such as burgers or shortbread, simply look more appetizing if they are neatly formed or have a motif stamped on them.

These tools compress mixtures into a flattish shape, sometimes embossing or sealing it in the process; otherwise they force the mixture through a nozzle or a specially shaped cutter. None of the tools are essential, unless you regularly ice cakes, but they are fun to use and do not cost the earth.

1 Burger press This cast-aluminium, cow-embossed, hinged press produces a compact, perfectly round burger. The press eliminates the air pockets that cause burgers to crack when turned.

2 Tortilla press As you pull down the handle of this ingenious press, two cast-aluminium hinged discs uniformly flatten a small ball of masa harina dough into a paper-thin tortilla.

3 Turnover press Making meat, fruit or vegetable turnovers is easy with this hinged, semi-circular, plastic press, which simultaneously moulds, crimps and seals the pastry.

4 Forcing bags Forcing bags are used in conjunction with a nozzle for piping semi-fluid mixtures that hold their shape. The bags are soft and pliable, and respond to the slightest pressure, so may require patience at first. These professional-quality bags are made of waterproof nylon and have a loop for hanging them up to dry.

7 Forcing/icing nozzles Used with a forcing bag or syringe, these conical nozzles shape the mixtures that are forced through them. Nozzles are made of metal, nylon or plastic, and come in a wide range of sizes and shapes. Those with well-defined, sharp edges produce the most clean-cut designs. Use them for writing or for piping decorative shapes such as stars, rosettes, ribbons or shells.

8 Icing syringe Icing is forced through the cylinder and nozzle by a plunger attached to a central shaft that passes through the lid. To operate the plunger, put your thumb through the central loop, hook your forefinger and middle finger through the loops on the lid, and press down.

5 Shortbread mould Beautifully and precisely carved, this hand-made sycamore mould embosses a traditional thistle design on top of shortbread. Sycamore is a dense wood that is particularly suitable for carving intricate designs and producing a crisp imprint.

6 Biscuit press There is no easier way to make biscuits than with this sturdy aluminium press. A plunger forces dough through a decorative cutter, producing flawless biscuits of various shapes. The gun is supplied with nozzles for piping fillings and decorations.

measuring

weight and volume

It was not until relatively recently that recipes began to specify exact amounts of ingredients. In the past, it was a matter of taking 'some' of one ingredient, throwing in a handful of this and a pinch of that, and heating 'until cooked'. Nowadays, though, we go to the other extreme and probably over-specify. To complicate matters, some cookbooks specify two, sometimes three, measuring systems: metric, imperial and American. However, the practice of using the dual imperial/metric system is gradually disappearing as more and more countries make a positive move away from the imperial to the metric system.

American recipes specify the majority of ingredients by mass or volume, even though measuring by weight is more accurate and in some cases easier. For example, how do you measure a cup of tomatoes? Or a cup of something that does not easily fit into the shape of a measuring cup? Recipes from other countries specify solid or dry ingredients by weight, and liquid ingredients by volume. Small amount of dry ingredients are also measured by volume, in teaspoons or tablespoons.

Measuring equipment is not expensive so it is worth investing in a set of scales and measuring jugs marked in imperial and metric measurements, particularly if you use recipes from different countries. You can then use either of the two systems; they are not necessarily interchangeable.

It is also worth buying several sets of measuring spoons, if only to save having to wash a single spoon each time you measure sticky or greasy ingredients.

When buying scales, the choice is between balance, electronic and spring scales – each has its advantages and disadvantages. Balance scales look great, but are fiddly to use. The weights are sold separately, and you will need to buy two sets if you use both metric and imperial measurements. Electronic scales are the most accurate type, but you will need to keep replacing the batteries. Spring scales are easy to use, but need to be well built – once the spring breaks they are useless.

When choosing measuring jugs, remember that a more accurate measurement can be obtained from a tall, narrow jug than from a wide one. A narrow shape causes the contents to rise higher up the jug, so there is a greater distance between the calibrations printed on the side. The wider the space between each increment, the easier it is to see when the contents reach a particular level. Clear jugs are more useful than opaque ones, as they allow you to see the contents at eye level.

1 Balance scales Made to a traditional design, these attractive scales work by force of gravity: when the ingredients in the pan weigh the same as the metal weights on the platform, the beam is horizontal. Balance scales are accurate and built to last, but they are not quite as easy to use as either spring or electronic scales. They are also somewhat unwieldy, so are best kept on the work surface for convenience.

2 Electronic scales Meticulously accurate, these state-of-the-art scales are good-looking enough to grace the most design-conscious kitchen. Their one slight drawback is that the control switch for changing the read-out from metric to imperial is on the underside of the base – other models have a more convenient push-button on top.

Measuring jugs

3 Invaluable in the kitchen, these tall polypropylene jugs can be used for measuring and pouring anything from a beaten egg to a large volume of stock. Very durable, they will withstand boiling liquids, and will not break if dropped. They are available in ¹/₂, 1 and 2.2 litre sizes.

4 This wide, 2 litre polypropylene jug can double up as a mixing bowl. It is especially useful for ingredients that need to be whisked, then poured in measured amounts – pancake batter, for example.

5 A small Pyrex jug is useful for transferring hot soup or stock from one container to another. It is heat-proof, easy to keep clean and will not absorb grease or smells.

6 Dry measuring beaker
The inside of this classic aluminium beaker is printed with different scales showing the equivalent volume of a particular weight of various dry ingredients. It also shows American cups and pints, English cups, pints and gills, as well as millilitres. The outside of the beaker is printed with metric/imperial conversions. Cheap, cheerful and extremely useful.

3

4

5

6

7 European measuring cups
These charming liquid measuring cups are made of aluminium and have finger-friendly handles. They hold 50ml, 100ml and 250ml.

7

8

8 American measuring cups
These stylish stainless-steel cups are used for measuring liquids. The top measurement is printed just below the rim of the cup so the liquid does not overflow. (Dry measuring cups are filled to overflowing and then levelled off with a knife.) They hold ¹/₄, ¹/₃, ¹/₂ and 1 cup.

9

9 British measuring spoons
Sensibly designed, these plastic spoons are narrow enough to reach inside spice jars. This comprehensive set includes the elusive ¹/₈ teaspoon and ¹/₂ tablespoon. It is worth buying at least three sets.

10

10 American measuring spoons
Made of heavy-gauge stainless steel, these measuring spoons are made to last. The set includes the hard-to-find ¹/₈ teaspoon. Buy several.

11 Diet scales A must for calorie counters, these scales accurately weigh very small portions of food, showing clearly whether or not that morsel of chocolate weighs 5 or 10 grams.

12

11

12 Spring scales Good looking and practical, these stainless-steel scales weigh up to 4kg of ingredients – about ¹/₂kg more than most kitchen scales. The dial is clearly printed with metric and imperial measurements, and large enough to read 20-gram or 1-ounce calibrations with ease.

temperature and time

Degrees and minutes matter. A few seconds can turn toasted almonds into blackened fragments; a few degrees can dry out a moist braise. Whatever the dish, it is always worth checking the oven temperature with a thermometer before starting to cook. Thermostats are notoriously inaccurate so you may find the actual temperature differs from the one you have set it to.

Spirit thermometers (with a graduated glass tube) are more accurate than spring-loaded ones (with a pointer). If you do decide to buy a spring-loaded thermometer, check that it is robustly made, as the spring is easily damaged.

Thermometers are also essential for food safety. Some foods, such as pork, chicken and microwaved meals, must reach a specific internal temperature to destroy harmful bacteria. A meat thermometer and a microwave thermometer are invaluable for checking this. Fridges and freezers need to be kept below specific temperatures to slow the growth of harmful organisms. As neither appliance will necessarily maintain the correct temperature, a fridge/freezer thermometer is a worthwhile purchase.

A timer with a loud ring is invaluable for reminding forgetful cooks that food needs checking or removing from the oven or hob. A timer is also invaluable if you are cooking several dishes at once, or if you have the type of oven that does not transmit smells to warn you that food is burning.

1 Candy/fat thermometer This well-made thermometer is designed for confectionery and for deep-fat frying. The probe is immersed in boiling liquid and held in place by a spring clip attached to the side of the pan. The thermometer has a movable red clip attached to the rim to make it easier to see if the pointer has reached the correct position.

2 Meat thermometer Though your senses will usually tell you when meat is cooked, a thermometer is useful for moments of doubt. Insert the probe so the tip is close to the centre of the meat. The meat is ready when the pointer moves to the appropriate wording (not shown). Like the candy/fat thermometer, it has a movable clip.

3 Spring-loaded oven thermometer As the oven heats up, a metal spring expands and moves the pointer. This one is sturdily made and is designed to hang or stand in the oven. It has a wide base to prevent it slipping between the racks.

4 Fridge/freezer thermometer This well-designed thermometer usefully indicates the optimum range of temperatures at which fridges and freezers safely operate.

5 Digital probe thermometer A digital readout and a fold-away probe are two useful features of this thermometer. It operates through an impressive range of temperatures – from minus 49.9°C to 199.9°C.

6 Microwave thermometer When defrosting food or cooking in a microwave oven, it is vital that the food reaches a safe temperature through to the centre. This plastic thermometer is specially designed so that it can be inserted deep into the food. The metal pin supplied with it is used to penetrate frozen food before the thermometer is inserted.

7 Water/chocolate thermometer The scale on this thermometer goes up to 60°C, which is the optimum temperature for tempering chocolate – the process of heating and cooling that stabilizes emulsified fats. The thermometer is also useful for checking the temperature of water intended to simmer rather than boil – in a bain marie, for instance. It is protected by a removable nylon cage.

8 Sugar/jam thermometer Made to a traditional design, this thermometer is indispensable when making jams and confectionery. It indicates the point at which sterilization takes place, and the stages in jam boiling and syrup making (wording not shown).

9 Spirit oven thermometer This is the most accurate and reliable type of oven thermometer. It shows heating zones as well as temperature (wording not shown), has a clear spirit tube and hangs or stands in the oven.

10 Rotary electronic timer This easily operated electronic timer is set by rotating the dial forwards or backwards to display the chosen time, and pressing the button. It counts upwards or downwards, has an insistent ring and will clip, hang, stand or magnetize according to your needs.

11 Clockwork timer With its resounding ring, this compact 60-minute timer is easily heard. It is also easy to use. It hangs by magnetism or by a convenient hook, and if you are venturing far from the kitchen, you can keep it on a string round your neck.

12 Hourglass timer Designed by Robert Welch, this is a classic, gravity-based timer for those who like their eggs cooked for exactly three minutes. An enamelled cast-iron frame protects the glass.

10

11

12

Egg boiling times

For best results, place an egg in cold water and begin timing the instant the water starts to boil.

At one minute the white starts to set, but the yolk is barely heated. A Caesar's salad dressing uses an egg boiled for one minute.

At three minutes the white is lightly set and creamy; the yolk is hot but still runny. French chefs call this an 'oeuf mollet'. This is the classic breakfast egg in which to dip your 'soldiers', or for serving in a bed of spinach, as in eggs Florentine.

At six minutes the white and yolk are set, but the centre of the yolk is very slightly creamy. Halved or quartered, these eggs make attractive garnishes. Halved eggs can be stuffed – remove the yolk, mix with your chosen seasoning and pile back in the egg.

At ten minutes the whites and yolk are tough, with a thin, dark line between the two. However, the whites and yolks can be rubbed through a sieve separately for use as a garnish – for veal schnitzels or Jewish chopped liver, for instance.

Jams and jellies Jams and fruit jellies set at just below 105°C, when the dissolved sugar interacts with the acid and natural fruit pectin. To test for set, spoon a sample of the freshly cooked jam or jelly onto a chilled saucer and after a couple of minutes push it with your fingertip – if a skin forms, it is set.

Sugar syrup Boiling sugar and water to make a syrup causes the water to evaporate, concentrating the density of the syrup. This is useful for sweet-making and for recipes that need different strengths of syrup. If you drop small amounts of hot syrup into iced water they form either a soft ball (at 115–118°C) or a hard ball (at 120–122°C).

Caramel Caramel is sugar syrup boiled until it reaches a temperature of 165–175°C, when it becomes medium to dark golden brown in colour, with a delicious toffee flavour. The syrup must not be stirred as it boils, but it can be gently swirled. When the caramel reaches the desired colour, plunge the base of the pan in cold water to stop the heat of the pan overcooking it.

storing

food

covering up

All food should be covered, regardless of where you store it. Leaving food exposed not only allows moulds and bacteria to get to work (and they do so even in the fridge), but also allows air, heat and light to destroy valuable nutrients. So, for the sake of your health, it is important to invest in suitable containers and get in the habit of using them.

Top of the list should be a collection of airtight polypropylene boxes. Buy several sizes and shapes: deep, shallow, large and small, remembering that square and rectangular boxes make more efficient use of available space than round ones. Buy self-adhesive labels so you can identify the contents easily.

Equally invaluable are foil and cling film. Both are handy for wrapping things tightly or covering bowls. Polythene bags are essential for sandwiches and for anything that needs gathering together in a flexible container.

Glass storage jars look attractive, but they are not airtight, nor do they protect the contents from light. They are suitable only for non-perishables such as dried pasta and pulses. Spices and dried herbs should be kept in airtight containers away from light. Nuts and wholemeal flour need airtight containers, too, as they contain fats that eventually become rancid if exposed to air. They also need protection from heat, so don't store these items in a cupboard close to a heating pipe or an under-unit strip light.

1

1 Polythene bags These are a household essential for wrapping sandwiches or for preventing moisture loss from fruit and vegetables while stored in the fridge. Heavy-gauge bags can be used for storing food in the freezer.

2 Aluminium foil Foil is used not only to protect food and pans during cooking, but also to exclude air during storage. Being flexible, it can be wrapped tightly round any awkwardly shaped items, such as a cooked chicken. Foil also keeps sandwiches fresh and prevents loose or chunky fillings from escaping. Unlike cling film, it does not cause cheese to sweat. Buy the heaviest grade possible – though cheaper, thin foil tears easily so what you save in money you waste in damaged foil.

2

3

4

4 Aluminium foil dishes Made from heavyweight aluminium foil, these are versatile containers in which to freeze, transport or reheat food. A flexible rim folds over a flat cardboard lid, which rests on the flattened edge. Though the foil containers are reusable, the perishable lids limit their useful life.

5 Foil bag Strong and flexible, this polythene-lined foil bag is ideal for freezing liquids such as soup.

5

3 Cling film Use cling film for tightly wrapping food or for covering bowls. Ordinary cling film should never be used in direct contact with very fatty foods, such as butter, high fat cheeses (e.g. Cheddar or Parmesan) or food in an oily medium (e.g. tuna in oil), as harmful substances in the cling film can migrate into the food. When covering bowls for use in a microwave, do not let cling film come in direct contact with the food unless the words 'Safe for use in the microwave' are printed on the packaging.

6 Cheese dome Cheese needs a cool temperature and circulating air during storage. This attractive glass dome keeps cheese fresh and moist while it is at room temperature. The wooden base has a channel round the edge to keep the dome in place.

Mesh covers

7 In pre-refrigeration days, an oval wire-mesh cover was used to protect meat from dust and flies. It allowed air to circulate round the meat, keeping it fresher than a close-fitting wrapping. Nowadays you might use it for refrigerated meat that you are allowing to come to room temperature before barbecuing.

8 This square nylon food umbrella can be used as temporary protection for any food that will fit under it. It can be folded flat when not in use.

9 Condiment jars These attractive jars are made of glazed stoneware and are traditionally used for potted goose and pork. Though not airtight, they do exclude light. They are best used for anything submerged in a protective liquid – such as olives in oil, or pickles in brine – and for dripping and lard. Straight sides, a wide neck and an easily removable lid make them easy to fill and reach into.

10 Garlic pot Garlic bulbs need access to air to prevent mould, and protection from light to stop premature sprouting. This pot provides both.

11 Preserving jar Certain foods will keep for months if they are vacuum packed in a sterilized container and submerged in a medium suitable for keeping bacteria at bay – acid, brine or oil, for example. This classic glass preserving jar fits the bill. It can be sterilized in the oven and has a rubber gasket and wire clip to seal the lid. The neck is wide enough for easy filling.

12 Butter dish A deep container is useful for protecting a block of butter while not in the fridge. This porcelain butter dish is good-looking enough to be brought to the table.

13 Stainless-steel container This airtight container has a well-fitting lid and is useful for storing cakes, biscuits or home-made muesli. It is smart enough to keep on the work surface.

14 Food boxes These versatile polypropylene boxes are suitable for the freezer, fridge, storecupboard, for picnics and packed lunches, and for reheating food in the microwave. Tightly fitting indented lids seal in smells, exclude air and facilitate easy stacking. When not in use, smaller boxes nest in larger ones, saving on storage space. They are available with different coloured lids for easy identification.

15 Enamelled bread bin This traditional bread bin is made of sturdy enamelled steel. It is not airtight as bread needs to be ventilated but kept dry. Remove all crumbs every few days to prevent mould. Wash and dry well every week or two.

16 Enamelled container Containers like these are not airtight, but they are suitable for storing items that are quickly used up and need to be easily accessible, such as sugar, tea and coffee.

sources

The following list will help you track down specific items featured in this book. Wherever possible we have given manufacturers so you can contact them to find stockists in your area (see 'manufacturers and distributors', page 141). If the manufacturers are unknown, we have given retail outlets from which the items can be bought (see page 142 for contact details). A number of items were obtained from the American retailer Sur La Table, which has a mail order service – Tel 001 800 243 0852.

Page

10 1 bread knife, 2 cook's knife, 3 utility knife, 4 tomato/sandwich knife, 5 paring knife and 6 vegetable knife by Zwilling J.A.Henckels; 7 knife block by Victorinox

11 8 V-shaped sharpener by Taylor's Eye Witness; 9 carborundum stone from David Mellor; 10 sharpening steel by Global

12 1 wooden chopping board from David Mellor, polyethylene chopping board from Divertimenti; 2 carving knife and fork by Le Creuset

13 3 ham/smoked salmon slicer by Lion Sabatier; 4 freezer knife by Gustav Emil Ern; 5 filleting knife and 6 boning knife by Zwilling J.A.Henckels; 7 'universal' cheese knife and 8 Parmesan knife from David Mellor; 9 grapefruit knife by Rösle; 10 oyster knife by Wüsthof Trident; 11 cleaver by Global; 12 and 13 Japanese knives by Yoshikin

16 1 swivel peeler and 2 Lancashire peeler from David Mellor; 3 Y-shaped peeler by Good Grips; 4 cannelle knife by Rösle, 5 citrus zester from David Mellor; 6 pizza wheel by Rösle; 7 cheese plane by Wüsthof Trident; 8 plastic bean slicer by Krisk; 9 metal bean slicer by Porkert; 10 hard-boiled egg slicer from Kitchens

17 11 black mandolin by Matfer; 12 wooden mandolin, 13 Mezzaluna and 14 hachoir from David Mellor; 15 chip cutter by Zyliss; 16 fish tweezers from Divertimenti; 17 fish scaler by Fox Run

24 1 kitchen shears from Pages; 2 kitchen scissors from David Mellor; 3 poultry shears from Kitchens; 4 apple corer and 5 courgette corers by Pedrini; 6 pineapple corer/slicer by Vacu Products; 7 melon baller and 8 cherry pitter from Fenwicks

25 9 bamboo skewers from Fenwicks; 10 kebab skewers, 11 small round skewers and 12 potato baking spike by Fox Run; 13 blue can opener from Lakeland; 14 can opener by Pedrini; 15 screwpull corkscrew by Screwpull® Le Creuset; 16 winged corkscrew by Pedrini; 17 lever-based corkscrew by Screwpull® Le Creuset; 18 'universal' opener from Lakeland

28 1 standing mixer by KitchenAid; 2 food processor by Magimix; 3 stick blender by Braun

29 4 blender by Waring; 5 juicer by Braun; 6 multipurpose kitchen machine by Bosch; 7 hand-held mixer by Kenwood

32 1 ceramic spice mill by Trudeau; 2 Crushgrind® spice mill by T.&G. Woodware; 3 meat grinder by Porkert; 4 metal pepper and salt mills from Divertimenti; 5 wooden pepper and salt mills by William Bounds

33 6 electric coffee mill by Krups; 7 perspex coffee mill from Habitat; 8 Parmesan mill from Pages; 9 nutmeg mill from Divertimenti; 10 metal pestle and mortar and 11 ceramic pestle and mortar from Kitchens; 12 Japanese pestle and mortar from author's collection

36 1 porcelain grater by Fox Run; 2 citrus grater by Sveico; 3 flat graters by Rösle; 4 box grater by Sveico; 5 Microplane® grater by Grace Manufacturing; 6 nutmeg grater from Pages; 7 rotary grater by Fox Run

38 1 tomato press from Habitat; 2 meat mallet/tenderizer by Fox Run; 3 garlic press by Bodum; 4 vegetable press from author's collection; 5 food mill and 6 potato ricer from Divertimenti; 7 potato masher by Good Grips

39 8 cone nutcrackers by Kitchen Craft®; 9 ratchet nutcrackers from Kitchens; 10 pincer nutcrackers by Pedrini; 11 lobster/crab crackers from David Mellor; 12 cone-shaped lime/lemon squeezer from Lakeland; 13 lemon reamer by Good Grips; 14 glass lemon squeezer from David Mellor; 15 chrome citrus press from Divertimenti

42 1 basic glass bowl by Bodum; 2 Duralex 9-piece set from Lakeland; 3 stainless-steel bowls by Rösle; 4 copper bowl from David Mellor; 5 melamine bowl by T.&G. Woodware; 6 ceramic bowl by Mason Cash

43 1 straight-edged spoon, 2 beech spoon and 3 boxwood spoon from David Mellor; 4 long-handled wooden spoon from Pages; 5 metal mixing spoon from David Mellor; 6 wire mixing spoon by

Rösle; 7 scoop from David Mellor; 8 insulated ice-cream scoop from Fox Run

44 1 salad dressing ladle and 2 portioning ladle by Rösle; 3 soup ladle from David Mellor; 4 Chinese wok ladle by Typhoon; 5 rubber spatula and 6 plastic spatula from Divertimenti; 7 coloured plastic spatula by Le Creuset; 8 wooden spatula from David Mellor

46 1 balloon whisk, 2 egg whisk, 3 twirl whisk, 4 spiral whisk, 5 jug whisk and 6 flat whisk by Rösle

54 1 flour and sugar dredgers by George East; 2 drum sieve by T.&G. Woodware; 3 flour sifter by Ekco

55 4 nylon sieve from Fenwicks; 5 and 6 bowl-shaped sieves by Rösle; 7 chinois sieve and pestle from Pages

56 1 cheesecloth by Ekco; 2 stainless-steel colander by Rösle; 3 long-handled colander from David Mellor; 4 enamelled colander by George East

57 5 pan drainer from Divertimenti; 6 perforated spoon by Paul Mitton/H. Faith; 7 tea strainer and 8 conical strainer by Rösle; 9 perforated skimmer from David Mellor; 10 wire skimmer from Pages; 11 noodle/pasta scoop from Divertimenti; 12 wire shaker by SEFAMA; 13 salad spinner by Zyliss

64 1 non-stick aluminium saucepan by Berndes; 2 stainless-steel saucepans by Cuisinox

65 3 anodized aluminium saucepans by Calphalon; 4 anodized aluminium milk pan by Meyer

66 1 stockpot with pasta insert: Le Pentole pot by ICM; 2 pressure cooker by Kuhn Rikon; 3 double boiler/casserole: Le Pentole pan by ICM; 4 copper saucepan from Divertimenti

67 5 preserving pan from Divertimenti; 6 slant-sided aluminium saucepan by Mermaid; 7 slant-sided anodized aluminium saucepan by Calphalon; 8 bain marie from Lakeland; 9 butter warmer by Rösle

69 1 polenta pan from Sur La Table; 2 zabaglione pan and 3 sugar boiler by Mauviel; 4 saucier by All-Clad; 5 cheese-fondue pot by Emile Henry

72 1 drip-filter coffee maker by Krups; 2 percolator by Cuisinart; 3 cappuccino creamer from Divertimenti; 4 traditional espresso maker by Pezzetti; 5 modern espresso maker from Aero; 6 plunge-filter coffee maker by Fox Run

73 1 whistling kettle by Alessi; 2 cordless kettle by Bodum; 3 traditional kettle by Le Creuset; 4 China teapot/tea press by Lakeland; 5 glass teapot by Bodum

74 1 couscousier by LI International; 2 three-piece steamer by Cuisinox; 3 bamboo steamers by Typhoon

75 4 rice steamer from Debenhams; 5 steaming trivet from Lakeland; 6 christmas pudding steamer and 7 fold-out steamer by Fox Run; 8 asparagus steamer and 9 fish kettle/poacher from David Mellor; 10 egg poacher from Lakeland; 11 'universal' steamer insert by Cuisinox

80 1 round frying pan from David Mellor; 2 wok by Typhoon; 3 ridged square frying pan from David Mellor; 4 stainless-steel sauté pan: Le Pentole pan by ICM

81 5 splatter screen by Ekco; 6 hard-anodized aluminium stir-fry pan by Meyer; 7 steel omelette pan by Rösle; 8 hard-anodized aluminium chef's pan by Meyer

82 1 crêpe/pancake pan and 2 oval pan by Matfer; 3 fajita pan by Calphalon; 4 blini pan by Matfer

83 5 Danish cake pan by Lodge; 6 karhai (Indian wok) from William Levene; 7 paella pan by Mayer; 8 chestnut pan by Fox Run

86 1 tempura pan from Habitat; 2 chip pan from Divertimenti; 3 potato nest fryers by Wirax; 4 electric deep-fryer by Magimix

89 1 toaster and 2 salamander from David Mellor; 3 blow torch by Kitchen Craft; 4 reversible grill by Lodge

90 5 flat stove-top grill by Typhoon; 6 circular wire rack from Sur La Table; 7 flat griddle from David Mellor; 8 waffle iron by SEFAMA; 9 ridged stove-top grill from David Mellor

92 1 long-handled fork, turner and tongs by Good Grips, basting brush by Fox Run; 2 oval portable barbecue by Lodge; 3 hibachi barbecue and 4 disposable barbecue from Woolworths; 5 wire holders by Fox Run

93 6 pedestal barbecue by SAEY; 7 kettle barbecue by Weber-Stephen Products

96 1 fish lifter from Divertimenti; 2 wok turner by Meyer; 3 fish turner by Rösle; 4 spring-action tongs from Lakeland; 5 scissor-action tongs by Fox Run; 6 angled turner by Rösle; 7 non-stick turner from David Mellor; 8 bamboo rice paddle and fork by Typhoon; 9 wire scoop and 10 turning fork by Rösle

98 1 double oven gloves, 2 enamelled self-basting roaster and 3 anodized aluminium roasting pan from Lakeland; 4 lifting forks from George East; 5 anodized aluminium roasting tray from Lakeland

99 6 porcelain fat separator from David Mellor, acrylic fat separator by Fox Run; 7 vertical chicken roaster by Fox Run; 8 trussing needle from Pages; 9 enamelled roasting pan from Divertimenti; 10 V-shaped roasting rack by Fox Run; 11 bulb baster by Ekco; 12 stainless-steel mini roasting pan from Lakeland

102 1 braising pan by All-Clad; 2 Brittany pot and 3 tagine by Le Creuset; 4 pot roaster by All-Clad

103 5 non-stick casserole by SKK Küchen- und

Gasgeräte; 6 enamelled Dutch oven by Le Creuset; 7 cast-iron Dutch oven and 8 brushed stainless-steel casserole by Hackman; 9 polished stainless-steel casserole by Taylor's Eye Witness

104 1 bean pot/fait-tout by Emile Henry; 2 marmite by Gres et Poteries de Digoin; 3 oval terrine by Emile Henry; 4 Tontopf pot from Lakeland; 5 round terracotta pot by Gres et Poteries de Digoin

108 1 rectangular ceramic gratin dishes and 2 oval ceramic gratin dishes by Emile Henry; 3 porcelain soufflé dishes by Apilco; 4 enamelled cast-iron egg dish and 5 enamelled cast-iron baking dish by Le Creuset; 6 porcelain ramekins, 7 porcelain oval gratin dishes and 8 porcelain chocolate pots by Apilco

109 9 earthenware potato baker by Gres et Poteries de Digoin; 10 glazed earthenware basins by Mason Cash; 11 cast-iron rectangular terrine by Le Creuset; 12 non-stick steel meat loaf pan from Sur La Table; 13 aluminium pudding basins from Pages

112 1 perforated pizza pan by George East; 2 pizza stone from Lakeland; 3 pizza peel/paddle by Fox Run; 4 ravioli tray, 5 pasta machine by Imperia; 6 wooden rollers, 7 pasta cutting wheels, 8 ravioli cutter from author's collection

117 1 brioche tin by Matfer; 2 non-stick bread tins from Lakeland; 3 non-stick French bread tin by Fox Run; 4 hinged tin by Le Creuset

120 1 joined small tins by Metalurgica; 2 foil and paper cups by Fox Run; 3 English bun tray and 4 Yorkshire pudding tray by Kaiser; 5 cooling racks by Wirax; 6 popover/muffin tray from Sur La Table

121 7 angel food cake tin from author's collection; 8 deep, round cake tins by Tathams Tinware; 9 springform tin by Kaiser; 10 Swiss roll tin by Le Creuset; 11 shallow cake tin by Kaiser; 12 madeleine tray from Pages

122 1 deep fluted tart tins and 2 shallow fluted tart tins by Le Creuset; 3 non-stick sponge tart tin by Kaiser; 4 tarte tatin tin by Mauviel

123 5 deep pie dish by Mason Cash; 6 pie bird by ICTC; 7 shallow pie dish from Lakeland; 8 pie plates from Sur La Table; 9 non-stick pie plate with insert from Lakeland; 10 aluminium baking sheet from David Mellor, blackened steel baking sheet by Bourgeat

126 1 dough scraper from Lakeland; 2 pastry wheel, 3 lattice cutter and 4 flexible palette knife from Pages; 5 pastry blender from Lakeland; 6 natural bristle pastry brushes by Kaiser; 7 rolled edged pastry cutters from Pages; 8 crinkle pastry cutters, 9 double-ringed doughnut cutter and 10 marble pastry board by Fox Run; 11 wooden rolling pin from Lakeland; 12 aluminium baking 'beans' by Matfer

128 1 giant ice-cube tray by Lékué Articulos Menaje; 2 fish mould from David Mellor; 3 ring moulds by Bradford Metal Spinning Co

129 4 bombe mould from David Mellor; 5 Charlotte mould by Le Creuset; 6 dariole moulds from author's collection; 7 heart mould from David Mellor; 8 large jelly/blancmange mould by Metalurgica, small jelly/blancmange mould by Fox Run

130 1 burger press and 2 tortilla press from author's collection; 3 turnover press by Fox Run; 4 forcing bags by Staines Catering Equipment; 5 shortbread mould from David Mellor; 6 biscuit press from Lakeland; 7 forcing/icing nozzles and 8 icing syringe by George East

132 1 balance scales from Divertimenti; 2 electronic scales by Soehnle

133 3, 4 plastic measuring jugs by Stewart; 5 Pyrex measuring jug by Ekco; 6 dry measuring beaker by George East; 7 European measuring cups from author's collection; 8 American measuring cups and 9 British measuring spoons from Lakeland; 10 American measuring spoons from Sur La Table; 11 diet scales by Fox Run; 12 spring scales by Typhoon

134 1 candy/fat and 2 meat thermometer by Fox Run; 3 spring-loaded oven thermometer by Kuhn Rikon; 4 fridge/freezer thermometer and 5 digital probe thermometer from Pages; 6 microwave thermometer by George East; 7 water/chocolate thermometer by Matfer; 8 sugar/jam thermometer and 9 spirit oven thermometer by Brannan

135 10 rotary electronic timer and 11 clockwork timer from Lakeland; 12 hourglass timer by Robert Welch Designs

138 1 polythene bags, 2 aluminium foil, 3 cling film, 4 aluminium foil dishes and 5 foil bag from Lakeland

139 6 cheese dome from Divertimenti; 7 wire-mesh cover by Wirax; 8 nylon food umbrella by Fox Run; 9 condiment jars and 10 garlic pot by Renault; 11 preserving jar from Lakeland; 12 butter dish by ICTC; 13 stainless-steel container by Rösle; 14 food boxes from Lakeland; 15 enamelled bread bin and 16 enamelled container by George East

manufacturers and distributors

This list should be used with the 'sources' list on page 140 to track down particular items featured in the book. Contact manufacturers for details of your nearest stockist. Where there is no UK office for a company we have given the distributor or importer, or the address of the main office abroad.

Alessi S.p.A.
Via Privata Alessi 6, 2282, Crusinallo (VB), Italy
Tel 00 39 032 386 8611

All-Clad Metalcrafters
424 Morganza Road, Canonsburg, PA 15317, USA
Tel 00 1 800 255 2523, 001 724 745 8300

Apilco
UK importer: F. Trauffler Ltd, 100 East Road, London N16AA
Tel 0207 251 0240

Berndes
UK importer: ICTC – see entry.

Bodum (UK) Ltd
Bourton Industrial Park, Bourton-under-Water Cheltenham, Gloucestershire GL54 2LZ
Tel 01451 810460

Bosch Domestic Appliances
Grand Union House, Old Wolverton Road, Wolverton, Milton Keynes, Buckinghamshire MK12 5PT
Tel 01908 328200

Bourgeat
Les Abrets, 38490, Isère, France
Tel 00 33 476 321 444

Bradford Metal Spinning Co. Ltd
Bradware Industrial Park, Leonard Street, Bingley, Yorkshire BD16 1DP
Tel 01274 511911

S. Brannan & Sons Ltd
Leconfield Industrial Estate, Cleator Moor, Cumbria CA25 5QE
Tel 01946 816624

Braun (UK)
Dolphin Estate, Windmill Road, Sunbury-on-Thames, Middlesex TW16 7EJ
Tel 0870 608 5555

Calphalon Corporation
PO Box 583, Toledo, OH 43697, 0583, USA
Tel 00 1 419 666 8700

Cuisinart
1 Cummings Point Road, Stamford, CT 06902
Tel 00 1 203 975 4600

Cuisinox
UK importer: ICTC – see entry.

Ekco Housewares
New House Farm Industrial Estate, Mathern Chepstow, Monmouth, Monmouthshire NP16 6UD
Tel 01291 638700

Emile Henry
UK importer: F. Trauffler Ltd, 100 East Road, London N16AA
Tel 0207 251 0240

Fox Run Craftsmen
Fox House, Stonedale Road, Stonehouse, Gloucestershire GL10 3SA
Tel 01453 828333

George East (Housewares) Plc
29 High Street, West Wickham, Kent BR4 0LP
Tel 0208 777 0444

Global
UK importer: I.Grunwerg Ltd
Silversteel House, 29–49 Rockingham Street, Sheffield SI 4EA
Tel 0114 275 6700

Good Grips
UK importer: Jim Wilkinson Promotions
Glenfield Park, Lomeshaye Business Village, Nelson, Lancashire BB9 7DR
Tel 01282 613644

Grace Manufacturing
UK importer: ICTC – see entry.

Gres et Poteries de Digoin
UK importer: ICTC – see entry.

Gustav Emil Ern
UK importer: M.Gilbert (Greenford) Ltd, Gilbert House, 1 Warwick Place, Warwick Road, Borehamwood, Herts WD6 1UA
Tel 0208 731 3700

Hackman
UK distributor: Dexam International Ltd, Housewares Section, Haslemere, Surrey GU27 3QR
Tel 01428 647601

ICM SpA
Via Don Minzoni 1, 25066 Lumezzane (Brescia), Italy
Tel 00 39 030 897 9011

ICTC
The Intercontinental Cooking & Tableware Co. Ltd
3 Caley Close, Sweet Briar Road, Norwich NR3 2BU
Tel 01603 488019

Imperia Trading
Corso Moncenisio 107, 10057 S. Anbrogio di Torino, Italy
Tel 0039 011 956 1377

W.F. Kaiser & Co. GmbH
UK importer: ICTC – see entry.

Kenwood Ltd
New Lane, Havant, Hants PO9 2NH
Tel 01705 476000

KitchenAid
UK distributor: Unit 21a, Monkspath Business Park, Highlands Road, Shirley, Solihull, West Midlands BN0 4NF
Tel 0845 601 1287

Kitchen Craft®
Thomas Plant (Birmingham) Ltd, 93–99 Holloway Head, Birmingham B1 1QS
Tel 0121 604 6000

Krisk
UK importer: R.G. Bennett & Co. Ltd, 60 Colney Road, Dartford, Kent DA1 1HU
Tel 01322 224258

Krups Sales Ltd
High Street, Tallaght Retail Centre, Dublin 24, Eire
Tel 01459 7977

Kuhn Rikon UK Ltd
Landport Road, Wolverhampton WV2 2QJ
Tel 01902 458410

Le Creuset UK Ltd
4 Stephenson Close, East Portway Industrial Estate, Andover, Hampshire SP10 3RU
Tel 01264 343909

Lékué® Articulos Menaje
c/Cadaques, 29-08120 La Llagosta (Barcelona), Spain
Tel 00 34 35 74 26 40

LI International Trading Co.
UK importer: Paul Mitton & Co./H. Faith – see entry.

Lion Sabatier
UK distributor: Le Creuset UK Ltd – see entry.

Lodge Manufacturing Company
6th Street at Railroad, P.O.Box 380, South Pittsburg, Tennessee 37380, USA
Tel 00 1 423 837 7181

Magimix UK Ltd
19 Bridge Street, Godalming, Surrey GU7 1HY
Tel 01483 427411

Mason Cash & Co. Ltd
Pool Street, Church Gresley, Swadlincote, Derbyshire DE11 8EQ
Tel 01283 217521

Matfer
UK importer: Paul Mitton & Co./H. Faith – see entry.

Mauviel
UK importer: ICTC – see entry.

Mermaid®
Samuel Groves
P.O. Box 1452, Hockley, Birmingham B18 5RG
Tel 0121 554 2001

Metalurgica
UK importer: Paul Mitton & Co./H. Faith – see entry.

Meyer (UK) Ltd
Morpeth Wharf, Twelve Quays, Birkenhead, Wirral, Merseyside L41 1LW
Tel 0151 650 6500

Moulinex Swan Holdings Ltd
35 Rocky Lane, Golden Cross, Aston, Birmingham B6 5RQ
Tel 0121 380 0500

Paul Mitton & Co./H. Faith
Unit 7, Trident Way International Trading Estate, Brent Road, Southall, Middlesex UP2 5LF
Tel 0208 574 1888

Pedrini PPL S.p.A.
UK importer: Newman Housewares
PO Box 62, Thornton Heath, Surrey CR7 8YJ
Tel 0208 653 9075

Pezzetti
UK importer: Thomas Plant (Birmingham) Ltd, 93–99 Holloway Head, Birmingham B1 1QS
Tel 0121 604 6000

Porkert
UK importer: Thomas Plant (Birmingham) Ltd, 93–99 Holloway Head, Birmingham B1 1QS
Tel 0121 604 6000

Renault
UK importer: ICTC – see entry.

Rösle
UK importer: M. Gilbert (Greenford) Ltd, Gilbert House, 1 Warwick Place, Warwick Road, Borehamwood, Hertfordshire WD6 1UA
Tel 0208 731 3700

SAEY
Industrielaan 4, B-9501 Kortrijk, Heule, Belgium
Tel 00 32 56 37 15 15

SEFAMA
UK importer: Paul Mitton & Co./H. Faith – see entry.

SKK Küchen- und Gasgeräte GmbH
D-41751 Viersen, Nettetaler Strasse 172–180, Germany
Tel 00 49 2153 89103

Soehnle Waagen AG
UK importer: Austin White (Northampton) Ltd, 3 Mansard Close, Northampton NN5 5D1
Tel 01604 588992

Staines Catering Equipment
Brent Road, Southall, Middlesex UB2 5LG
Tel 0208 574 2322

The Stewart Company
Stewart House, Waddon Marsh Way, Purley Way, Croydon CR9 4HS
Tel 0208 686 2231

Sveico
UK importer: Paul Mitton & Co./H. Faith – see entry.

T.&G. Woodware
Unit 9a–10b, Old Mill Road, Portishead, Bristol BS20 7BX
Tel 01275 841841

Tathams Tinware
20 Forest Business Park, South Access Road, Walthamstow, London E17 8BA
Tel 0208 520 5206

Taylor's Eye Witness
Harrison Fisher & Co. Ltd, Milton Street, Sheffield, S3 7WJ
0114 272 4221

Trudeau
UK importer: F .Trauffler Ltd, 100 East Road, London N16AA
Tel 0207 251 0240

Typhoon Products
Adams House, Dickerage Lane, New Malden, Surrey KT3 3SF
Tel 0208 942 9361

Vacu Products
Unit 32615, Roshock Trading Estate, Droitwich, Worcestershire WR9 0LR
Tel 01299 250480

Victorinox
UK distributor: Burton McCall, Victorinox House, 163 Parker Drive, Leicester LE4 0JP
Tel 0116 235 1111

Waring
UK distributor: Robot Coupe (UK) Ltd, 2 Fleming Way, Isleworth, Middlesex TW7 6EU
Tel 0208 232 8171

Weber-Stephen Products (UK) Ltd
Suite 4–10, Croston House, LE Business Park, Leyland, Lancashire PR5 1TZ
Tel 01772 458580

William Bounds Ltd
UK importer: ICTC – see entry.

William Levene Ltd
167 Imperial Drive Harrow, Middlesex HA2 7JP
Tel 0208 868 4355

Wirax Wirewares Ltd
Warstock Road, Kings Heath, Birmingham B14 4RW
Tel 0121 474 2212

Wüsthof Trident
UK distributor: A.J. Boulton Ltd, Unit 11, Far Green Industrial Estate, Hanley, Stoke-on-Trent, Staffordshire ST1 6AZ
Tel 01782 207755

Yoshikin
UK importer: I.Grunwerg Ltd, Silversteel House, 29–49 Rockingham Street, Sheffield SI 4EA
Tel 0114 275 6700

Zwilling J. A. Henckels
UK distributor: Dexam International Ltd, Housewares Section, Haslemere, Surrey GU27 3QR
Tel 01428 647601

Zyliss
UK distributor: Dexam International Ltd, Housewares Section, Haslemere, Surrey GU27 3QR
Tel 01428 647601

retailers

This is a selection of good retail outlets. The list is organized by region for ease of use, but note that many outlets offer mail order. As well as specialist shops, it is also worth trying the cookshops within department stores such as Debenhams, Fenwick, Habitat, Heals, IKEA, John Lewis, Liberty and Selfridges, some of which have branches nationwide. Lakeland is listed under Northern England but has shops throughout Britain – see entry.

LONDON AND SOUTH EAST

Aeromail (Mail Order)
46 Weir Road, London SW19 8UG
Tel 0208 971 0066
www.aero-furniture.com
Selected range of kitchen tools and cookware.

Anything Left Handed
57 Brewer Street, London W1R 3FB
Tel 0207 437 3910
Knives, ladles, lifters, turners, zesters and peelers for the left handed.

Aria
295–296 Upper Street, London N1 2TU
Tel 0207 704 1999
An emporium for Alessi fans, carrying the full range of pans, kettles, coffee machines and other iconic items.

Bodum
24 Neal Street, London WC2 9PS
Tel 0207 240 9176
71–71A King's Road, London SW3 4NX
Tel 0207 376 3825
Unit 22A, Whiteleys Shopping Centre, Queensway, London W2 4YQ
Tel 0207 792 1213
www.bodum.com
Ovenproof glassware, coffee and tea makers, insulated jugs, tableware.

The Conran Shop
Michelin House, 81 Fulham Road, London SW3 6RD
Tel 0207 589 7401
55 Marylebone High Street, London W1M 3AE
Tel 0207 7723 2223
www.conran.co.uk
Selected housewares, kitchen tools and cookware.

Cucina Direct (Mail Order)
PO Box 6611, London SW15 2WG
Tel 0208 246 4300
www.cucinadirect.co.uk
Comprehensive range of kitchen tools and cookware.

David Mellor
4 Sloane Square, London SW1W 8EE
Tel 0207 730 4259
Professional kitchen tools, cookware and tableware. Mail order available.

Divertimenti
139–41 Fulham Road, London SW3 6SD
Tel 0207 581 8065
45–47 Wigmore Street, London W1H 9LE
Tel 0207 935 0689
www.divertimenti.co.uk
Superb range of kitchen tools, cookware, housewares and tableware.

Elizabeth David Cookshop
Hanningtons, 1–10 North Street, Brighton BN1 1GJ
Tel 01273 729560
Nasons, 46–47 The High Street, Canterbury CT1 2SB
Tel 01227 456755
Excellent range of all kinds of kitchen tools and cookware. Mail order available.

Gill Wing
190 Upper Street, London N1 1RQ
Tel 0207 226 5392
Comprehensive range of kitchen tools and cookware.

Jerry's Home Stores
163–167 Fulham Road, London SW3 6SN
Tel 0207 581 0909
American-style kitchen tools, cookware, housewares and tableware. Mail order available.

Kooks Unlimited
2 Eton Street, Richmond, Surrey TW9 1EE
Tel 0208 332 3030
16 Eton Street, Richmond, Surrey TW9 1EE
Tel 0208 940 8448
Professional kitchen tools, cookware, cake decorating equipment, oven-to-tableware.

Ocean Home Shopping
9 Hardwicks Way, London SW18 4AW
Tel 0207 670 9083
www.oceancatalogue.co.uk
kitchen tools and cookware. Mail order only.

Pages
121 Shaftsbury Ave, London WC2H 8AD
Tel 0207 565 5959
www.pagescatering.co.uk
Professional kitchen tools, cookware and catering equipment, and tableware. Mail order available.

SOUTH WEST

Kitchens (Catering Utensils)
4–5 Quiet Street, Bath BA1 2JS
Tel 01225 330524
167 Whiteladies Road, Bristol BS8 2SQ
Tel 0117 973 9614
Comprehensive range of professional kitchen tools, cookware and catering equipment.

Outdoor Chef
Triflo House, Mill Road, Barton St David, Somerton, Somerset TA11 6DF
Tel 01458 851234
www.outdoorchef.net
Gas-fired kettle barbecues with specialist cooking systems for pizza, paella etc. Good range of tools and accessories. Mail order available.

EAST ANGLIA

Elizabeth David Cookshop
22 Fitzroy Street, Cambridge CB1 1EW
Tel 01223 321579
See entry under London and South East.

Marchants Cookware
7 St John's Street, Bury St Edmunds, Suffolk IP33 1SQ
Tel 01284 705636
An Aladdin's cave of professional kitchen tools and cookware, run by cooks for cooks. Mail order available.

Williams and Griffin
152 High Street, Colchester, Essex CO1 1PN
Tel 01206 571212
Professional equipment for the home cook.

MIDLANDS

Abraxas Cookshop
Heart of the Shires Shopping Village, nr Brockhall, Weedon, Northamptonshire NN7 4LB
Tel 01327 342335
Excellent range of professional kitchen tools and cookware, based in a converted farm complex.

Cheltenham Kitchener
4 Queen's Circus, Cheltenham, Gloucestershire GL50 1RX
Tel 01242 235688
Professional kitchen tools, cookware and catering equipment. Mail order available.

David Mellor Country Shop
The Round Building, Hathersage, Hope Valley, Sheffield S32 1BA
Tel 01433 650220
See entry under London and South East.

Elizabeth David Cookshop
51 Mill Lane, Solihull, West Midlands B91 3AT
Tel 0121 709 2302
See entry under London and South East.

Kirklands The Cookshop Ltd
North Walls, Stafford, Staffordshire ST16 3AD
Tel 01785 259960
Professional tools and cookware for the home cook.

The Original Cookware Company
8 Silver Walk, St Martin's Square, Leicester LE1 5EW
Tel 0116 251 2842
Professional tools and cookware for the home cook.

Robert Welch Studio Shop
Lower High Street, Chipping Campden, Gloucestershire GL55 6DY
Tel 01386 840522
19 Old Square, Warwick CV34 4RU
Tel 01926 400422
www.welch.co.uk
Ironware, glassware and cookware. Mail order available.

NORTHERN ENGLAND

Barkers
198–202 High Street, Northallerton, North Yorkshire DL7 8LP
Tel 01609 772303
Department store with very large selection of items for the kitchen.

Cook's Corner
2 Fairfax Court, Yarm, Cleveland TS15 9Q2
Tel 01642 783729
Small shop crammed with everything you could wish for in the kitchen.

Lakeland Ltd
Alexandra Buildings, Windermere, Cumbria LA23 1BQ
Tel 015394 88100
www.lakelandlimited.com
Outstanding mail order company selling enormous range of kitchen tools and cookware, tableware and housewares. Also branches for personal shopping at Aberdeen, Bluewater, Cardiff, Chester, Chichester, Edinburgh, Exeter, Glasgow, Guildford, Harrogate, Ipswich, Lincoln, Peterborough, Stratford-upon-Avon, Truro, Tunbridge Wells, Windermere, Worcester and York.

Peter Maturi and Sons
84–86 Vicar Lane, Leeds LS1 7JH
Tel 0113 245 3887
Professional kitchen tools and cookware with good range of knives.

SCOTLAND

The Cook's Shop
21 High Street, Banchory, Grampian AB31 5TB
Tel 01330 825511
A specialist shop for the enthusiastic cook.

Pots and Pans
Unit 25, Howgate Centre, Falkirk FK2 1DN
Tel 01324 638245
Sauchiehall Centre, Sauchiehall Street, Glasgow G2 3ER
Tel 0141 331 2836
Professional kitchen tools and cookware for the home cook.

Ross Cookshop
Unit L7, Princes Mall, Princes Street, Edinburgh EH1 1BQ
Tel 0131 557 4097
11 Queen Street, Glasgow
Tel 0141 204 4900
Professional kitchen tools and cookware with a good range of bakeware.

Studio One Cookshop
71 Morningside Road, Edinburgh EH10 4AY
Tel 0131 447 0452
Professional kitchen tools and cookware for the home cook.

WALES

Kitchens (Catering Utensils)
14 High Street, Cardiff CF10 1AX
Tel 02920 229814
See entry under South West.

Peppercorns
5 King Street, Llandeilo, Carmarthenshire SA19 6BA
Tel 01558 822410
Professional kitchen tools and cookware.

IRELAND

Brown, Thomas and Co.
88–95 Grafton Street, Dublin 2
Tel 00 353 1 6056666
Department store with kitchen tools and cookware section.

Captain Cook's Homestore at Moores
9–11 Church Street
Coleraine, Londonderry
Tel 028 703 44444
Also branches at Ballymena, Lisburn, Portadown, Portrush. American-style cookshop selling wide range of professional kitchenware for the home cook.

La Cucina
63 High Street, Holywood, County Down BT18 9AQ
Tel 02890 422118
Unit 15, Fairhill Shopping Centre, Ballymena, County Antrim BT43 6UF
Tel 02825 658800
Professional kitchen tools and cookware for the home cook.

WEBSITES FOR ONLINE SHOPPING

The Cook's Kitchen
www.kitchenware.co.uk

eCookshop
www.ecookshop.co.uk

Gourmet Cookware
www.gourmetcook.co.uk

index

publisher's acknowledgements

We would like to thank the following
for contributing recipes to this book:

Page
15 Ken Hom: 'Hong Kong-style broccoli
and baby corn', © Ken Hom 2000;
19 Anne Willan: 'summer squash
salad', from *Anne Willan's Burgundy*,
Weidenfeld and Nicholson, © Anne
Willan 2000
30 Charlie Trotter: 'macadamia nut-
crusted chicken breast with coconut-
lemongrass emulsion', © Charlie
Trotter 2000
35 Das Sreedharan: 'coconut vegetable
stew', © Das Sreedharan 2000
45 Jill Dupleix: 'risotto with red wine
and sausages', © Jill Dupleix 2000
60 Alain Ducasse: 'pumpkin and
girolle soup' and p62 'chicken stock',
from *Ducasse Flavours of France,
Artisan*, © Alain Ducasse 1998
61 Emi Kazuko: 'ramen with pork and
vegetables', © Emi Kazuko 2000
76 Paula Wolfert: 'Tunisian couscous
with greens, red peppers and garlic',
from *Mediterranean Cooking* (revised
edition), HarperPerennial, © Paula
Wolfert 1994
84 Raymond Blanc: 'scallop and
shiitake sir-fry', from *Blanc Vite*,
Headline, © Raymond Blanc 1998
85 Madhur Jaffrey: 'chicken in a red-
pepper sauce', from *Madhur Jaffrey's
Quick and Easy Cookery Course*, BBC
Books, © Madhur Jaffrey 1997
90 Rose Gray and Ruth Rogers:
'grilled squid with chillies', from *The
River Cafe Cookbook*, Ebury, © Rose
Gray and Ruth Rogers 1995
94 Wolfgang Puck: 'barbecued seafood
skewers with sun-dried tomato basil
aïoli and grilled vegetable salad', ©
Wolfgang Puck 1993
95 Peter Gordon: 'slightly smoky
grilled quails with ginger, mirin, basil
and sesame', from *Cook at Home with
Peter Gordon*, Hodder & Stoughton,
© Peter Gordon 1999
100 Jamie Oliver: 'pork and
crackling', from *The Naked Chef*,
Michael Joseph, © Jamie Oliver 1999
105 Claudia Roden: 'chicken tagine
with preserved lemons', from
Tamarind & Saffron, Penguin Books,
© Claudia Roden 1999
110 Alice Waters: 'fresh shell bean
gratin', from *Chez Panisse Vegetables*,
HarperCollins, © Alice Waters 1996
Reprinted by permission of
HarperCollins Publishers, Inc.
114 Marcella Hazan: 'ricotta and mint
tortelloni', from *Marcella Cucina*,
HarperCollins, © Marcella Hazan 1997
118 Ursula Ferrigno and Eric Treuille:
'Swedish dill bread', from *Bread*,
Dorling Kindersley, © Ursula Ferrigno
and Eric Treuille 1998

author's acknowledgements

I would like to thank Jacqui Small for
asking me to write a book about one
of my greatest passions. Thanks and
appreciation to my editor, Stuart
Cooper, for his good humour, guidance
and support throughout the project,
and for his calmness in moments of
crisis; and to my husband, Ed, for his
generosity of spirit in allowing me to
put the book before everything else.
  I am deeply indebted to Jude
Austin of the Bath branch of Kitchens,
without whom the initial research
would never have got off the ground;
to Susan Campbell for kindly allowing
me to use information from her own
book *The Cook's Companion*; and to
Michael Michaud and Robert Welch
for their help and support. Thanks
also to Roz Denny for contributing
to the techniques pages; to Robin
Rout for designing a beautiful book;
to Mark Williams for the photography;
to Josie Frater for locating the props;
to Pippin Britz for preparing food for
photography; and to Alexandra King
for testing the recipes.
  My appreciation and thanks also go
to the chefs and food writers who
contributed recipes.
  For their particular patience
in lending countless items for
photography, special thanks to the
retailers David Mellor, Divertimenti,
the Bath branch of Kitchens, and
Lakeland Limited. Thanks also to All-
Clad Metalcrafters, the Calphalon
Corporation and Sur La Table for
shipping items from the US. I am
also grateful to the following UK
companies for lending numerous
items: Dexam International, Fenwicks,
Fox Run Craftsmen, George East
(Housewares), The Intercontinental
Cooking & Tableware Co., Meyer,
Paul Mitton & Co./H. Faith, Liberty,
Newman Housewares, Pages, Robert
Welch Studio Shop, F. Trauffler,
Typhoon Products; and to the following
public relations companies: the Grayling
Group for Le Creuset items, Parker
Hobart Associates for Divertimenti
items, Rawlingson Lane Publicity for
Rösle items, Reader Communications
for Good Grips items.